Alone
and
Beginning
Again

Alone and Beginning Again

Nancy Karo Johnson

Judson Press ® Valley Forge

ALONE AND BEGINNING AGAIN

Library of Congress Cataloging in Publication Data
Johnson, Nancy Karo.
  Alone and beginning again.
  Bibliography: p.
  1. Johnson, Nancy Karo. 2. Baptists—United States—Biography. 3. Death. 4. Grief. 5. Remarriage. I. Title.
BX6495.J52A32   286′.1′0924 [B]   81-20702
ISBN 0-8170-0951-5   AACR2

The name JUDSON PRESS is registered as a trademark in the U.S. Patent Office.
Printed in the U.S.A. ✜

Dedicated to:
My Family—
My "Blended" Family

Foreword

Nancy Johnson is a gracious, vivacious, outgoing person—
a beautiful friend for whom I thank God. I am grateful that
she has gone through the struggle of writing this book. I vividly
recall being in the Karo home not long before Nancy's husband,
Lindon, died. He had struggled for months with cancer, even
preaching during the closing months of his life. Now I could
feel a sense of heavy anguish in that home, but deeper than that
a quiet, powerful faith. It was apparent that Christ was in this
home. I left renewed, grateful that Lindon and Nancy had invited me to come.

This book, really a testimony of faith, is an honest sharing of
feelings and deepening insight growing out of the ending of
Lindon's life in this world, and the struggle that followed for
Nancy. We need this kind of integrity about our feelings in the
church. For too long we have covered up or tried to evade those
tides that run in the depths of our life. We have held back or
been afraid or turned away from one another. So much of church
life has been superficial. Consequently our congregations have
been sterile and flat. Yet the Bible is full of emotional honesty.
As the Psalmist says: "Out of the depths have I cried unto Thee,
O Lord." Or Jesus, facing the Greeks, said: "Now is my soul
troubled, and what shall I say?" So Nancy has risked sharing
with us, her readers, both her weaknesses and strengths. That
is a precious, trembling gift. And we can learn so much from
this.

But she has also given us simple, helpful suggestions. Any
one of us can reach out to someone suffering, we can listen or
touch or quietly pray. And there is healing in that. This does
not require professional lingo or special training. So perhaps
some of us will be encouraged to move out in a new way because

7

of the suggestions we find here.

In the end there is also the gift of love that comes to Nancy Karo and Emmett Johnson, a friend and counselor of long standing to both Nancy and Lindon. Then they are married—another one of the Lord's beautiful serendipities. And she tells of the joy of a new beginning for both of them, which is not without some very real struggle and pain. So, dear reader, let this book speak to you and then pass it along.

—Roger Fredrikson

Contents

Preface

L ife can be good again.

I have gone through the experience of losing my husband by death, through the ordeal of grief, and now I feel good about life—about me.

Single the second time around: There are more people facing that situation every year because of death or divorce.

No one had prepared me for what might lie ahead, so our family muddled through. We came out whole. Most people do. But some things could have been avoided or gone through with more grace and understanding had I been prepared.

After my experience as I spoke or led workshops, my focus gradually changed from "Death and Dying" to "Helping the Hurting: The Formerly Married." People began asking, "What is losing a spouse like? What can we do if we are faced with that situation? How long does it take to feel better? Does the pain ever stop?" And finally, "Won't you write about it?" Both my parents and my husband continued prodding and encouraging me along this line.

". . . The God whose consolation never fails us! . . . so that we . . . may be able to . . . share with them the consolation we ourselves receive from God" (2 Corinthians 1:3-4) had always been meaningful but became more so now that I had shared one of life's deepest experiences.

God's consolation had not failed me. I could share that with others. That is what I would like to do. In this book I include quotations from my personal journal kept throughout my experiences.

This is my story, with the insights of others who understand the process of going from death or divorce through grief to life again—endings and beginnings.

Endings

Basically, I guess I'm a softie. I see a sad movie and, throughout the movie, I struggle to conceal tears. I hear about the abuse of children and can't listen to details because I cry too much. Why, I even cried when we recently purchased a live lobster. I was astute enough to realize that *I* couldn't be the one to place it in boiling water. But then I lifted the lid too soon to check on it!

I dislike moving. More times than I care to remember, I have sobbed uncontrollably while saying good-bye. I grew up in a godly home and had a close family relationship. Leaving for college—a mere thirty miles away from home— caused tears.

I met my husband when he and I were members of a gospel team, now called "The Evangelism Corps," affiliated with the Baptist General Conference. Six months after the end of our second year with that group, Lindon Karo and I married. I cried as we left Minnesota for California where we spent the first two years of our married life and where our oldest son, Steve, was born. Try to explain tears to a young husband all set for a glorious honeymoon!

Leaving California after two years, to embark on Lin's college education—tears. You'd have thought I had lived there all my life. And we were returning to *my* hometown and family!

While Lin was still in college, our second son, Rob, was born. Soon after that, Lin became pastor of a small mission church in southern Minnesota. Because I was young—maybe naive is a better word—I don't think I faced the struggle some seminary wives face today: the fear of the "role" of a pastor's wife. I didn't know I was to play a role. I guess I was what we now term "my own person."

As a pastor's wife I became extremely involved in the church, even more so than I had been as a layperson. My husband was involved with the entire congregation, and I became involved with some of the women there and in the community who became close friends.

Being a pastor's wife naturally meant moves. So with moves came painful experiences: leaving my close friends in the church and leaving my neighbors whom I had seen almost daily. I do not leave a place gracefully. Maybe you have experienced something similar; you are trying to be ever so brave when inside you feel ripped apart. All someone has to do is say a kind word and the tears flow. This happened with me. The more I cried, the more embarrassed I became, and the louder the sobs became. I always felt sorry for the people around me who stood by helplessly, yet with compassion, as I cried and cried.

Our third son, Scott, was born in 1969 with hyaline membrane disease. I was warned that he would get worse before he got better, and that *if he lived* for forty-eight hours longer, he would recover fully. Some might see those words as words of hope and cling to them. I didn't. I only heard, "He might die!"

Scott lived. I learned later what James meant when he said, "Count it all joy, my brethren, when you meet various trials . . ." (James 1:2, RSV).

Moves, job losses, moves of close friends, painful experiences can prepare us for that ultimate loss. In August of 1972 my husband of eleven years was diagnosed as having lymphosarcoma.

Cancer.

> [The doctor] simply announced that Lin had lymphosarcoma. We had never heard the word before but the ending of it, 'sarcoma,' had an ominous sound. His explanation was businesslike: 'Worse than Hodgkin's disease, but better than leukemia. . . .'
>
> Questions! How do you ask questions when your mind is in turmoil? Two weeks ago Lin had seemed vigorous and healthy, a thirty-one-year-old man at the peak of physical prowess. Was [the doctor] now saying that Lin would die? Or be permanently hospitalized? Was he through as a pastor?
>
> We finally collected ourselves enough to ask a few questions and how they would treat this disease. The young intern told what he knew about the disease but said he didn't know the treatment. However, he assured us they would start something. After the doctor left, we sat looking at each other. We were so shocked we barely knew what to say.[1]

The words I recorded in my journal were:

Tuesday, August 15, 1972. Stunned, shocked, tearful, speechless, unbelieving, all at once. I sobbed and sobbed leaving the hospital and broke again telling Marilyn and Bob (friends taking care of the boys). I had to tell the boys and struggled so with that. I finally said, "Dad has cancer and will begin taking medicine that we are praying will work. And, of course, God can heal him, too. We don't know." Steve asked, "Will Dad die?" "We don't know for sure, but let's really pray."

The next day the specialist and his assistants did explain quite carefully the chemotherapy that Lin would receive (seven different pills, four times daily), the side effects (loss of hair, nausea), and that the treatment would continue indefinitely.

I do know that I experienced a grieving process even prior to his death seven months later.

Elisabeth Kübler-Ross speaks of denial as one of the stages that dying people face. Lin and I both experienced denial. Hearing that your loved one has cancer is not something for which you are prepared. How else can your whole being respond, but to deny it? Possible death as a result of cancer goes against life! Against our hopes, our dreams. Against our love for each other. I believe it was through that shock, that unbelief, that denial, that my psyche, my emotions, my very self were prepared to handle what was to be that ultimate loss.

Chemotherapy began the morning after we were given the diagnosis. The months that followed brought long, long days and nights when God was so very near—and times when he was out of sight completely.

The ups and downs I faced at times were unbearable. Three weeks after the original diagnosis, Lin appeared to be in remission. We were elated. That elation lasted a short five weeks. I wrote:

October 16 . . . Lin began to feel quite ill, with headaches and much pain. By Tuesday, the right side of his face was beginning to feel numb and his fingers tingled. On Wednesday evening, he called to me in distress, "Come quickly," He was seeing everything double. We immediately called Dr. Taddeini [his specialist]. He told Lin to come to the hospital the next morning. He sounded concerned.[2]

Then,

On October 26, when Lin had been back in the hospital for a week,

Dr. Carl Christenson and Gordy Lindquist [friends] were visiting one evening and suggested that I go with them for coffee and a piece of pie. That night Carl told me that Lin's situation was deteriorating. The drugs were not doing what they were expected to do. His condition was now called lymphosarcoma leukemia in the acute stage. "Lin has about a fifty-fifty chance," Carl said. . . . That night I felt absolutely helpless. What did the future hold? How long did Lin have? What could I tell Steve and Rob? "Help, God! Help!" was all I could say.[3]

December of that year was a particularly difficult time. Lin's blood count was all out of whack and just before Christmas he got the flu. He was in the hospital most of December with weekend passes so he could be home with the family and preach on Sundays. During one difficult week I remember praying with passion and then relating my experience to our boys. "Let's not fool around. Let's *really pray* that God will heal Daddy." Scott, now three, yelled, "Yaaay. Then I can climb on his back and wrestle!"

It got worse.

Lin was home for Christmas, but the flu got worse, the boys got sick, and I wondered how much longer I could carry on. I prayed then that God would keep me well until Lin's mom arrived in early January. Was I thankful when that day arrived. Help had come.

Then Lin's mother got sick!

"Lord?"

But I never did get sick.

I recently reread the first chapter of 2 Corinthians as I began writing this book. Verse 10 says ". . . and *he will deliver us again*, he on whom our hope is fixed" (italics added). He does—again and again! When you know you can't stand any more, God is there to deliver. I was able to carry on, with strength. Colossians 1:11 says, "May he strengthen you, in his glorious might, with *ample power* to meet whatever comes with fortitude, patience, and joy . . ." (italics added). Even though that joy sometimes lagged behind, fortitude was there. Being a stubborn Swede may have helped some, too!

January was a "down" month; Lin spent all but the last week in the hospital. February he was home and able to resume the basic pastoral duties of the church. But he was admitted for the last time into the hospital at the end of February because of bleeding in the urinary tract. He was given a pass to preach— two weeks before his death.

Near the time of Lin's death, we experienced more aggravation. It seemed that our entire congregation, and even some people in the wider state conference, knew before we knew that Lin's condition was worsening. Lin had the *right* to know his prognosis; it was his body being afflicted. Yet we seemed to be the last to find out.

I am a firm believer in being told all the facts. I guess being a Christian is a distinct advantage in being able to handle this.

I was glad that from the first Lin and I were told together about his having cancer. There were no games we needed to play with each other like trying to hide the truth, *acting* as though nothing were wrong. The advantage in being told the truth was that we both could work through our fears of death and go on with life.

A week before Lin's death, a doctor friend and Lin's specialist talked to me about the seriousness of his condition and, being honest with me, tried to prepare me for the inevitable. That day still seems only a short time ago. I can see myself sitting in that cold hospital office, feeling so small and helpless, yet waiting until I left to burst into sobs. My college roommate, Annette, was a social worker at that hospital and had been with me now daily for the last seven months. I turned to her, knowing she would listen—and care.

People were there when I needed them, sometimes to say they were praying, sometimes to stop and pray with us, sometimes to eat with me, and sometimes just to squeeze my arm or give me a hug. I needed people.

On March 21, 1973, Lin died. I knew when I returned from lunch that this would be the last day he would be with me. By evening when his condition was grave, they wanted to give him oxygen. He balked at that. We had both fully agreed that there were to be no heroic last effort life-support systems. At least he could die with dignity.

Since Lin's death I have read much about cancer, about death and dying, and about grief. I even wrote a book about death. One thing I have frequently noticed in my explorations is the concern that people be allowed to die with dignity.

The dying person deserves to continue to be a part of decision-making in the home (child-related decisions, purchases, the car, etc.) and even in the hospital (the care received, the decisions to take or not to take chemotherapy or pain relievers).

The dying person deserves to have family and loved ones

nearby for emotional and physical support. Family members can offer the most support when it is needed at times when the dying person wants honest answers to questions asked or simply needs comfort from those closest to him or her.

The Philadelphia Inquirer, September 6, 1979, had an article entitled, "Readers Agree: There's a Time to Let Live, Time to Let Die." In that article, the mother of a twenty-three-year-old, a victim of a rare type of cancer said, "In four years, I saw him age from 19 to 90. During that time he fought courageously, accepting all treatment and hoping to beat the odds. For a while it looked as though he might make it. His youth, no doubt, was a factor in his battle to live, and yet a day came when he told me: 'Mom, there comes a time when life and death become equal.' At the end we asked only what was necessary to keep him comfortable."

Another recounted her experience: "My parents, when they became terminally ill, died with the same peace and dignity with which they lived, thanks to a consistently watchful, loving family and doctors who cared. . . ."

A nurse said, "The most important thing to do, I feel, is to let that person know, through words and touching, that someone is there who cares."

When the doctors were telling me of the gravity of the situation that week before Lin finally died, I asked if I could take him home. I have to give those doctors credit for pondering that question for the time they did. They answered that they could not allow me to do that because I would not be able to handle it. They were right.

I had three boys at home, the oldest ten. My mother was there too. But that last week was harder than I had imagined. Lin's physical needs could have been met and cared for only where he was—in the hospital, surrounded by caring doctors and nurses and a whole lot of friends! But I would much rather have had him home, to die in comfortable surroundings with family, than in a hospital room.

Lindon Karo died quietly on March 21, 1973 at the age of 32. Friends were with me. My dad was with me. Emmett Johnson, the executive minister of the Minnesota Baptist Conference, a pastor to pastors, was there. Both he and his wife, Darlene, helped Lin and me so much during Lin's illness. People prayed. People cried. But no amount of support could make any sense of his death. I read Psalm 69:1-3 that night:

Save me, O God;
for the waters have risen up to my neck.
I sink in muddy depths and have no foothold;
I am swept into deep water, and the flood carries me away.
I am wearied with crying out, my throat is sore,
my eyes grow dim as I wait for God to help me.

And wait . . . and wait . . . and wait.

Caring for the Dying

Most people have heard about Elisabeth Kübler-Ross's five stages of dying. Many can recite them. Few understand them as they relate to a dying person or the family of the dying.

We faced most of the stages.

Denial. This happens when a person is first told she or he is dying and says, "No. It can't be. Not me!" Lin faced that the day after he was told he had cancer. I faced it to some extent.

Anger. "Why me?" Many face their impending death with strong anger: anger at God, anger at the family. Think about it. How would you feel if you were leaving everyone and everything you had ever known? Anger, perhaps?

Bargaining. "Yes, me, but. . . ." The only bargaining I recall Lin doing was in the month he died when he prayed, "Lord, keep me here until the boys are grown."

Depression. When the person comes to the point when he or she says, "Yes, me," the person often becomes depressed.

Acceptance. Lin was in and out of acceptance the entire seven months of his illness. Always there was a hope that healing would occur or a cure might come. Hope is all-important. One *may* die with hope but almost surely, without hope, one *will* die. Lin's final acceptance came one and one-half hours before he died when he said good-bye to me and to those with him that night. Most people reach the acceptance stage and reach it early. Few die still denying death. And most die a peaceful death.

I was glad to be with Lin when he died and I know he wanted me there. He struggled to live, but he died at peace, quietly.

There are fears faced by the dying which I understand better now. A common fear is, "Will death be painful or frightening?"

Fortunately, today pain can be relieved and the patient can be comfortable. Doctors and nurses are becoming more understanding and are not so adamant in following protocol: an injection every *four* hours. Lin's last day was his most uncomfortable. The four-hour limit was lifted when I asked that he receive an additional injection *two* hours later so pain would be relieved.

"Will I be alone when I die?"

In the past the dying were placed in the terminal ward of the hospital. Doctors and nurses avoided patients or ignored their cries for help. Now families are encouraged to visit. Visiting "hours" are lifted for spouses. Children can visit. Loved ones can be with the person and help during those difficult times. Not only did it help Lin to have me there when he died, but being with him also helped me and aided in my grieving process. I was there when he needed me most.

Other fears are losing control of bodily functions, the loss of dignity; being unable to care for the family, and concern for their future welfare; the fear of losing everyone and everything dear to the person. Comfort for the believer comes in the belief of the eventual reunion—a celebration with God and our loved ones who have died before.

The fear that concerns us the most is the fear of the unknown. We know this life. Even the worst times we are able to cope with and understand somewhat. As believers in life after death, we know we will have a home with Christ. We believe it to be a state of peace, contentment, joy, fun, learning, growth. Still, it is unknown. We have not experienced it and can talk personally to no one who has. Christ has lived on earth and now is seeing us through life. We know our home with Christ is to be better, that He is there. But it is unknown. For other fears, we have some answers. But not for this fear.

A Christian physician tells of visiting one of his patients. "I don't want to die: tell me what lies on the other side." The doctor quietly answered: "My dear sir, I wish I could tell you, but I do not know." they talked a little while about the mystery of it all and then bade each other good-bye. As the doctor opened the door to depart, a dog sprang into the room and leaped on him with delight. Turning to the sick man, the doctor said: "Did you see that? This is my dog. He has never been in this house before. He did not know what was inside here. He knew nothing except that his master was here, and so he jumped in without fear. I cannot tell you what's on the other side, but I know the Master is there—and that's enough. When he opens the door, I expect to pass without fear into his presence."[1]

Our hope is in Christ and the validity of his Word: Hope in

the resurrection. After death *is* resurrection. Lin died in peace knowing that. Some day, so will I.

How can I help someone who is critically ill? Many ways.

The ministry of presence is one important way to say "I care." You can visit at the home or in the hospital. Stop by for a few minutes to say you care.

Listen. Listening means involvement. Hear what the person is saying. Let that person talk, complain, ask questions. Listen for cues: "It's not too busy around this place at night."

"I'll bet that's a lonely time for you. Say, could I come and stay with you on into the night?"

In 1976, both Emmett Johnson and his wife, Darlene, were diagnosed as having cancer. When Emmett was in the hospital, a friend of his, Delmar Dahl, was with him. He came to visit him with books to read and things to do and stayed all night— reading if Emmett slept, listening when he needed to talk, getting the bedpan or a glass of water. Delmar was available. Delmar was also available a month later when Darlene died. The ministry of presence is one of the greatest ministries Delmar or anyone could have given.

Say something. If you do not know what to say, say, "I don't know what to say. . . ." An honest response leaves the door open for the other to respond and begin a conversation. It shows that you do care. Or you could say, "I don't know what to say, but I want you to know that I care." Maybe add a squeeze of the hand or arm!

Nurses seem to be ministers to the dying. They dare to talk, ask questions, show emotion, and listen, as do the cleaning persons who are daily in the room. Many doctors attempt to remain uninvolved; they see many die. Yet one of my most moving experiences occurred the day Lin was dying. His intern, not on duty that day, stayed close by and sat at the station on Seven South weeping. He cared.

Pastors are expected to say things. They are the "professional" pray-ers. When pastors are honest about their own feelings, they become more credible to the dying person. At times the dying person will open up with a professional. The pastor can elicit a response from the dying person and thus bring about communication others have failed to.

Send cards. Everyone likes mail. When you send a card, be sure you write a note on it. You could mention why you are sending this particular card, or that you have been thinking about and praying for the person and wanted to send a card to show you care. Cards mean much more if there is a note. One woman wrote to us, "I'm storming the gates of heaven for you." That meant something!

Help with practical things. This helps the dying person and his or her family. As I visited Lin daily in the hospital, I let the housework go. The people of our church, Salem Baptist, came over twice and thoroughly cleaned the house. The exterior of the parsonage needed painting; two men in the church did that. People offered to baby-sit. Others took care of the car for us. And my mother was available to answer the telephone to give me time to rest or just to be alone.

What can you do? Stop and think about what needs doing around your home—lawn care, snow shoveling, taking care of the heating system. It may be something simple for you but overwhelming for the person lying in a hospital bed worrying about neglected chores.

One area of service which is often overlooked is that of food. Hospital food gets awfully boring. Fresh fruit or a home-baked item can be a great "perker-upper."

Allow for the expression of feelings. Touch is important, too. One man came in to see Lin and just threw his arms around him, both of them weeping openly. Lin hadn't cried before this. His friend's hug and tears opened Lin up to be able to do the same. He began to cry openly. So did my dad! It's good to see men able to cry.

I have an excerpt from the book *Where Have All the Children Gone? Gone to Grown-ups, Everyone.*

> Grown-ups don't cry. They don't do it if they fall down hard and get skinned up on the outside. They don't even cry if they get hurt on the inside, like when your best friend tells you he's only your second-best friend. Maybe grown-ups can't cry.
>
> I know they have tears though. I saw one once on my daddy's cheek. He was watching "Bonanza" on television. He didn't know I saw it. I think he was nervous trying to figure out what to do with it.
>
> I wonder what happens to all the tears inside of grown-ups. Does the hurting part just stay inside of them?[2]

I think it does.

If you allow for that expression of emotion, if you cry with your friends who are dying, they can cry with you. They will feel better. You will feel better. This open show of emotion will open up communication. Tears are important. Hugs are important, a squeeze on the arm, or a touch. *I* needed hugs. Suddenly I didn't have my husband to hug me very often. Our assistant pastor, Lee Eliason, was a hugger and he would give me big hugs. I needed that.

On a list of "don'ts" would be: Don't come in with "God's answer" to the whys or a long exposition on God's will for suffering. These things are worked over almost daily in the dying person's mind; they constitute an ever-present dilemma. What is needed most is your caring, not a discourse.

In Leslie Weatherhead's book *Why Do Men Suffer?* there is an illustration I like:

> When they are making a Persian rug, they put it up vertically on a frame, and little boys, sitting at various levels, work on the wrong side of it. The artist stands on the right side of the rug, the side on which people will tread, and shouts his instructions to the boys on the other side. Sometimes a boy will make a mistake in the rug. I have a Persian rug in my possession, given me by an Arab sheikh whose guest I was for some time in Mesopotamia. The pattern of the rug suddenly develops a yellow irregularity. Indeed, such asymmetry in design is a mark that a Persian rug was made in Persia and not in Wolverhamptom! I said to the student, "What happens when the boy makes a mistake?"
>
> "Well," he said, "quite often the artist does not make the little boy take out the wrong color. If he is a great enough artist, he weaves the mistake into the pattern."
>
> Is there not here a parable of life? You and I are working on the wrong side of the rug. We cannot watch the pattern developing. I know I put in the wrong color very often. . . . Sometimes I am tempted to say, "Is there Anybody on the other side of the rug; am I just left to make a mess of my life alone? Is there *Anybody* there?" Then, through the insight which comes back with returning faith, I realize that instead of making me undo it all or letting my life's purpose be ruined, God puts more in. . . . So, at the end, when he calls me down off my plank and takes me round to the other side, I shall see that just because he is such a great Artist, no mistakes of mine can utterly spoil the pattern; nothing can divert his purpose ultimately, or finally spoil his plan.[3]

We don't see the finished side. We see all those horrible loose ends. And they don't make any sense.

A dear friend, Paul Greely, had fought leukemia for six years. Then it appeared that the cancer was winning. He and his wife, Liz, struggled courageously. It didn't make any sense at all that Paul wouldn't get to go to medical school and graduate like his best friend, Keith. Paul's mother said, "Keith is graduating, but Paul will go to a different graduation." No, it didn't make any sense in our mind's eye. Paul, a terrific guy with a great zeal for life, a fantastic sense of humor, an influence wherever he went, was dying so young.

This past Christmas the hospital where he and his wife were employed had as their Christmas letter the love story of Liz and Paul Greely—a witness to their faith in Christ in the face of these seemingly horrendous circumstances.

We see the wrong side of the tapestry!

A verse that has meant so much to me speaks of the Lins and Pauls and Darlenes we know. "As for David, when he had served the purpose of God in his own generation, he died . . ." (Acts 13:36).

Help, I'm Alone

A widow! What an awful word. A widow? Now what?
Funeral to arrange.
Casket to purchase.
People to notify.
Calls to be made.
And tears to be shed.
Shocked.
Numb.
"No!"
Restless.
Sleepless.
"Please help, God!"

"I am wearied with crying out, my throat is sore,
my eyes grow dim as I wait for God to help me" (Psalm 69:3).

Lin's going to come back. No. Yes. No, he won't.
My mind was not functioning. I was discombobulated. Confused.

". . . I am poor and needy;
O God, hasten to my aid.
Thou art my help, my salvation;
O Lord, make no delay" (Psalm 70:5).

I couldn't sleep. I would rest awhile, then wake up, going
over the same things night after night.
". . . He carries us day by day . . ." (Psalm 68:19). Good. Day
by day. Remember, day by day.
I had to hurt in order to heal.
Sleeplessness: Waking. Wanting your mate. Sleep again—
awake again.
"Please God, help me!"

As I was struggling through my own set of emotions on the morning after Lin's death, I knew I still had to tell the boys. Ten is young to be fatherless, and Steve was the *oldest* of the three; Rob was seven and Scott, three. It was so hard to say, "Your dad died last night. He is in heaven now. . . ."

During that period of *shock* and *numbness* and *denial,* I did things by rote. I think even the boys did, young as they were. There were no arguments, no disagreements. Numb. I knew I needed to help them and I didn't even know how to help myself.

My mom and dad were there to help. I don't know how my mom did all she did in those days because her pain was about as deep as mine. Dad and Emmett Johnson helped as I went to the funeral home to choose a casket and make those arrangements. People brought in food; even the grocer brought a casserole! All of this was so helpful those first few days.

After the funeral, reality struck! *Pain.*

You have heard people say that the pain feels like someone is twisting a knife inside. That is an accurate description. Yet there is also an emptiness. It is an enigma: pain, yet emptiness.

That pain is as real for the grieving person as it is with someone who has had a leg amputated. The leg is gone, the nerve endings are not. There is pain where the limb once was. Scripture says, ". . . the two shall become one. . . ." (Matthew 19:5) That is what happens in marriage. When one partner leaves either through death or divorce it is as though part of oneself is destroyed. How true! The "we" became me. Now our decisions were mine alone (a horrible revelation for one of the worst decision makers!).

Some people become physically ill upon the loss of a partner, and I can understand why. Philip W. Williams, a medical doctor, says, "There can be dizziness, blurred vision, rashes, palpitations, chest pains, shortness of breath, general aching, heavy menstrual periods, fainting, indigestion, and other symptoms."[1]

Going to bed—*our* bed—was the hardest. I went alone. I'd cry over and over, "He's not here. He's not coming back." I would say it aloud, think it, feel it, and try to talk myself into that fact. I'd cry until I wondered if there were any tears left. I actually woke myself one night crying. I had heard of crying oneself to sleep, but waking oneself?

Waking in the middle of the night. Reaching over. No one there. Pain. Excruciating pain. No one there, but feeling his presence.

Three years after Lin's death, Emmett Johnson's wife, Darlene, died. One night after her death he thought he heard a noise. He woke up and said, "Aren't you feeling well?" She had been there for so long. So dependable. Now, no one.

Two weeks after Lin's funeral, my dad and I took a trip to Arizona to visit with my sister Judy for a few days, and then we drove to California. It was good to get away from responsibilities and memories for a time.

I was first asked to share my experience in California, at the Willow Glen Baptist Church. Being accustomed to public speaking, I accepted, but it was more difficult than I had anticipated. When I stood up, my mouth went dry, my tongue would not work. I was sweating. But there was healing here, too. God's people in that church had been praying for both Lin and me ever since they first heard he had cancer. They had continued to pray—and write—after Lin's death. There was a bond there and an affirmation to me that I was loved and cared for. And I had taken *a step toward getting back to normal activities.*

At Willow Glen Baptist Church I met Grandma Fiscus, who had been a special friend of my parents for some time. She provided a key to my recovery. A woman in her eighties, she *still* prays for the boys and me. In Grandma Fiscus I saw a godly, compassionate person who walked with Christ. Upon my return home, I received her letter with words that were ever so comforting: "I'm praying that God will wrap cotton around your heart!"

Oh, did I need that cotton! Something to soften the pain—a buffer. Then I read Psalm 125:2: "As the hills enfold Jerusalem, so the Lord enfolds his people, now and evermore." The cotton! My cry so often would become, "More cotton, Lord."

After that two-week vacation, I felt more refreshed and ready to get on with living. The days seemed to be going better, though the nights were still unbearable at times. I could keep busy during the day, but my thoughts would wander at night. No one was there. Memories were vivid. The pain was very evident and intense.

Then one day I began to realize that even though the pain was there, and maybe just as severe, it was *less frequent.* As always, friends were close by to help me during my bad days. Nights weren't as easy. It was during those times I would write in my journal and invariably turn to Scripture—usually the Psalms where I found someone else hurt as deeply as I. And then I could go on. The times between each painful experience began to stretch. This gave me hope.

Good Friday, April 20, 1973. Well, I came home today. I don't know—maybe the journal should end here and I really should get on with the task of living. Tonight Psalm 106:2 says, "Who will tell of the Lord's mighty acts and make his praises heard?" Me! Then verse 4: "Remember me, Lord, when thou showest favour to thy people . . ." I'd really appreciate it, Lord.

I felt it was about time he showed favor to *me*. Then. . . .

Saturday, April 21, 1973. Date-wise, one month ago that Lin died. Tonight I took his shirts off hangers, to use the hangers for my clothes. I felt ripped apart. I didn't think I would react like that (most of the clothes had been gone since soon after the funeral). "I need that cotton tonight, God."

I read a bit of *Psalms Now*. In Psalm 142 a paragraph read, "God deliver me from my prison of loneliness. Turn my cries of distress into proclamations of joy. Direct my steps into the fellowship of others who love and serve You."[2] Talk about a good paragraph! The latter has been done, but the first sentence needs a little doing! I remember, though, what Lin said the night I told him how bad his condition was (the week before he died). First, he was so distressed in leaving Scotty, Rob, and Steve, and then he said, "But there's nothing we can do about it. I'll have to face it." He then talked about going on with life. There's nothing I can do now about Lin being with God. That's great for him and I really do mean that. I'm lonely, but God can help with the cotton!

Easter Sunday came a month after Lin's death. I mentally prepared myself for this day. Actually, I prepared for all of those big firsts: anniversary, birthday, Christmas. It wasn't nearly as bad as I had anticipated. It was only when the congregation sang "Crown Him with Many Crowns," that I couldn't sing.

That evening in our church service there was the usual time of sharing. I finally got up enough courage to stammer my way through what I wanted to say. I mentioned how God was working in my life, and then I tried to explain that I had needs. I was lonely. It was hard to say, "I need help." But people aren't mind-readers and who would tell them if I didn't? When they were made aware, they responded!

By now I could see that I was *back to normal activities*. Not that there weren't bad days, but the initial shock was gone; the constant, intense pain was gone; and those painful times were less frequent.

Hope!

I read Psalm 119:49-50, on April 27.

> Remember the word spoken to me, thy servant,
>   on which thou hast taught me to fix my hope.
> In time of trouble my consolation is this,
>   that thy promise has given me life.
> This is God's promise, his consolation, and hope.

I was still saying "we" will do this, or "he *is*" and I continued to keep that present tense alive for some time. One man said that his wife had died two years before, but he still had moments when it seemed that she really hadn't died. Those flashes occur but they don't last.

Looking back, I see there were times when I was also quite excited about what was happening; I was growing. I wrote:

> Friday, May 4, 1973. I've thought a lot about Lin today and our time together but it didn't bring the depression I felt Monday and Tuesday. Yaaay! I was reading Psalm 139, which is familiar to me, but verse 8 stood out. "If I climb up to heaven [my high points, my exuberant feelings], thou art there; if I make my bed in Sheol [my depressed, lonely, painful experiences], again I find thee." God, You find me and lift me up every time. Verse 17: "How deep I find thy thoughts, O God, how inexhaustible their themes!" There is not an emotion I've experienced that isn't matched by a verse of Scripture, *every* time. Then verse 23 says, "try me." I feel I've been *tried* over and over again these past eight and a half months since Lin's cancer was diagnosed. I'm ready for a rest, Lord!

Now something else occurred to me. It was so good to have the lonely days farther apart and *not be so severe*. It was those sneaky things that got to me, like a look that reminded me of my husband or the time the church had a picnic and played ball. The last time they had done that, Lin had played, hitting the ball *over* the trees! It was those things in between important dates that I wasn't prepared for.

I remember the first Bible study I attended after Lin's death. We had always attended together, but I felt I could handle going alone now. When I arrived, I realized our group was having its annual fish fry. Everyone was there from the last fish fry—except Lin. It was one of those situations in which that uncomfortable "feeling" permeates the group. I couldn't wait to leave.

I shared this with one of the women a few days later. She asked me why I hadn't told them of my feelings so they could have ministered to me. I should have. We could have all cried together and then had a good fish fry. Instead, it was a strained time with no one saying much.

Another of those "sneaky" times happened when I was in California visiting my close friends Dan and Nancy Baumann.

Thursday, April 19, 1973. What a day. First, listening to the "shop-talk" between Dan and Maurie (two pastors) was almost unbearable because it was so much a part of my life with Lin.

Second, golfed in the afternoon. I could hardly take it at first. Lin and golf were synonymous during the summer. Just last summer we had vacationed with the Baumanns and golfed together.

Third, saw *Camelot*. Good movie but the ending was a bit difficult for me with his, "Good-bye Jennie." Just too much thinking back when Lin said, "Good-bye, Honey," and was gone a couple of hours later.

May 24, 1973. I know I never will understand Lin's death fully, but I am fully aware of God's sovereignty, His love, and His care for me.

Yesterday I was thinking of how every new situation has always been better and surely God won't be letting us down now. He does have something—a surprise—that I haven't counted on but that will be a great thing spiritually, I'm sure.

A friend of mine, Marlys Moline, had lost her husband a year or so before Lin became sick. She had once said to me, "I thought I would never be happy again, and one day I woke up happy." I remembered those words. I mulled them over many times. And you know, one day, I, too, *woke up happy*. The time for healing was slow, so slow that it wasn't perceived. Then one day that inner peace, joy, and happiness were evident. I was alive. I was whole. I knew I had made it. I had gone through the shock, that time of emptiness and physical pain, the time when the pain became less frequent and finally less severe; and I returned to normal activities. I got back to life! I joined the human race again, and I joined life. There were painful times. Yet those painful times brought growth. They brought a new awareness of God, his people and his Word.

I had joined life; yet I thought of those going through another form of grief, the pain of divorce. Many do not want divorce and are caught in it. Even if the marriage was "bad" and divorce seemed to be a release from an unbearable situation, the grief process—the letting go—is there.

After their marriage, "Edie and Bill" shared their experiences with Richard Krebs, author of *Alone Again*. Edie said, "You know, I can still see my first husband standing on the front porch the morning he left, saying, 'I'm doing you the biggest favor of your life.' [Obviously, Edie did not share his feelings.] He was, too, because if he hadn't left, I wouldn't have met Bill."[3]

The author explains further, "God has been involved in Edie's and Bill's lives. He was involved with them before they even knew each other. He accompanied them through the process of letting go of their first marriages. He continued to be involved with them as they met and married each other."[4]

Alvin Rogness says, "Grief is as universal as death. Sometimes it cripples. Occasionally, it enables."[5]

When I read Job 42:12, "Furthermore, the LORD blessed the end of Job's life more than the beginning . . .," I jotted alongside that verse, "I guess this can be true even though now it doesn't look that way. Hang in there, Nancy." I did. And he did!

CHAPTER

4

Warning Signals
(Types of Grief)

To me, grief is a combination of the painful emotions accompanying the loss (whether by death, divorce, or separation) of someone or something dear to me.

> Why do we grieve? . . . First of all, we grieve for ourselves. We are sad because we are suddenly, painfully deprived. We ache because we are separated from someone we love and need. . . .
> Second, there is fear. Our world has changed suddenly, and we do not know what is ahead. . . .
> And third, there is insecurity . . . the solid earth under your feet is crumbling, and you have nothing to hold on to.[1]

Personalities play a part in how we handle painful situations and setbacks. Our backgrounds vary. Grief is relative to each one passing through its grip. It has emotional and psychosomatic symptoms: pain, emptiness, tightness, sweating, chills, depression, restlessness or inactivity, sleeplessness or sleepiness. On and on the list goes.

Recently I attended the funeral for our friend, 26-year-old Paul Greely. As I was riding to the grave-site with friends, one in the car asked, "Has your attitude toward death changed since Lin died?" "No," I responded. "I had no 'attitude' concerning death before. It has been *since* his death that I have dealt with death, struggled through grief, and come to life."

Another said, "The one good thing about Liz [Paul's widow] is that they didn't have any children." I responded with, "And the hardest thing now for Liz is that they didn't have any children."

Liz didn't have the care and concern for little ones, but she also had no children who were a living part of Paul. She had no one to care for, no noise in the house, no regular, everyday, people noises.

There is no *easy* hurt. One doesn't hurt less because one does or does not have children. For each person grief is unique. Grief is the result of an *intense* loss.

Grief has been defined as sadness, distress, sorrow, hurt. The *American Heritage Dictionary* gives as its definition for grief: "Intense mental anguish, deep remorse, acute sorrow." I agree with the addition of those adjectives. Grief is not only distress; it is *intense, deep, acute* distress. It involves deep emotions, not surface emotions. Sorrow. We do not sorrow as those who have no hope, but we do sorrow.

We may have an assurance that we will meet our loved one again, but we want things as they were and know they will never be that way again.

In reading books on grief and in talking with others, I have come to the realization that my situation was not the "worst," although I surely felt it was. I thought I hurt worse than anyone had ever hurt before. Anyone who is going through grief because of death or divorce, feels that way.

Something we love and cherish and do not want to give up is taken away. Even in divorce a part of us is gone. It may not have been a healthy situation, but it is gone. We must get on with the task of putting ourselves together and begin living again. We are again reminded of the amputee who still feels that limb that is no longer a part of him or her. We want to communicate and cannot.

I realized that my feelings were not really weird, as I had thought. The waves of sorrow that I thought lasted for hours and hours, when they only lasted for about twenty minutes, were not uncommon. I thought I was never going to get over that deep hurt, that intense pain.

When entering a room full of people, some people in grief want to leave for fear someone will say something that will start them crying, and they will be unable to stop. It is easy for a grieving person to want to stay away from social occasions. He or she feels there is something wrong with him or her, that he or she is not "normal."

What is "normal?"

Philip Williams wrote about *shock*. Shock is normal. "God has built into us this natural buffer for the initial blow. It is a good gift because it protects us. . . . Shock numbs us and gives us time to get ready for our bereavement journey."[2]

I like the word "gift." Shock does protect us. We need that

gift of time. This is similar to the denial that a person faces when told he or she has cancer. Denial is as natural for a grieving person as for one who is dying. "No, it can't be!"

I went through a period of *restlessness.* Restlessness is also normal. People did not notice because I am naturally an active person. They would have noticed had I been doing what was not normal for me—sitting home doing nothing. Those active days helped me get through. I had friends around who asked me to lunch, and I took them up on it every time.

Another normal reaction is that of *guilt:* "If only I had gone to the hospital sooner." "If only we had caught some warning signals." "If only I hadn't been so angry that last time." "If only . . . ."

One woman had an experience that she related to me. One evening she and her husband were going to a banquet. He bought a corsage for her and brought it home. She immediately let him know that she was *not* going to wear a corsage. "No one *ever* wears corsages at these banquets!" Besides that, he had come home late, making them late for the banquet only because he had stopped to buy that stupid corsage. She left it at home. Guess who sat across from her? Someone wearing a corsage! A few weeks later her husband had a heart attack and died a short time later. To her, "If only I had worn that corsage" was a statement of monumental guilt.

"If only . . ." statements are universal.

My "if only" happened the night Lin died. Many people were there: my dad, Emmett Johnson, Lee Eliason, Annette. I remember saying to Lin, "You're such a great man!" If only I had said, "I love you." But I didn't. "If only . . ."

Emmett went through a similar experience with his guilt.

Shortly after his wife died, he was going through some of her belongings. In her purse was a card saying, "Things I Don't Like About Bud." As he read those things, he had to admit that he was guilty of them. But Darlene was dead. He couldn't ask for her forgiveness. There was nothing he could do. However, he knew he *could* rely on the grace of God.

In times like that, that is all one can do. God is good. His grace is sufficient and he will forgive. He will take care of the eternal end of it! Emmett had to rely on the God who does forgive and the God who heals. He settled it with God.

Emmett then happened to turn the card over and he remembered where it had come from—a conference where participants were asked to state "things I like and the things I don't like about . . ." The other side of the card listed "The Things I Like About Bud." And that list was longer!

Through the grace of God there was forgiveness. There was affirmation. There was healing.

Psalm 119:41 says, "Thy love never fails; let it light on me, O LORD . . ." In some of those difficult times, "Thy love never fails; let it light on me!"

Anger is also normal.

A person in grief may feel anger toward the physician: the doctor might not have tried everything possible. Maybe one of the newer tests could have caught the cancer sooner.

Or the thought occurs: "How can a God of love let a thing like this happen?" God takes the brunt of more anger than any person. One feels He is responsible. "He is the Giver of Life. How about being the Sustainer of life!" "Couldn't He keep my loved one alive a while longer for me?" God gets the anger and the blame.

One may get angry at the loved one, angry at the person who died, or who left, as in divorce. "If you hadn't died (or left), I wouldn't be in the mess I'm in."

My anger was never directed at God. I guess I had received so much care from God, that anger at God didn't occur to me. I never figured out the "why" but God was with me during the experience. It wasn't until several months after Lin's death, when I was going through a particularly difficult time, that I remember just screaming out, "Why did you die? I wouldn't be in this situation if you hadn't died!"

The Christian community can be critical of people such as I who get so angry. "They aren't handling this very well. They shouldn't be angry like that." Whether or not I *should* have felt anger is beside the point. I did.

The question one needs to ask is "What would I do if I were in that situation? How would I be feeling?" Anger is okay and, in fact, there can actually be comfort in anger.

> To feel angry is natural, normal. To be angry is a potential part of the healing process. This is a part of being a bereaved Christian. To suppress anger and never let it out can lead to a deeper than normal depression.
>
> We may be angry at God. It is hard to accept that life is unsure and that death is an uncertain certainty. These thoughts make us feel powerless. Being angry is a natural, desperate attempt by us

to control the order of things, since God seems to have let us down.[3]

Anger at God is normal. We have a big God. He can handle it!

Depression occurs when things mount up, nothing goes right, and one is all alone. It is a normal reaction, but it certainly did not feel normal to me. It was a feeling that caused me concern, but I found that it, too, passed. It would come and go, but it didn't overwhelm me when I realized that it was not a permanent part of my life. After all, I was now alone. That was new to me and many of my feelings were also new.

The feelings of depression and other feelings that I encountered helped me and helped my whole emotional system, my psyche, to get through the task of grief.

Grief becomes harmful when a person allows his or her emotions to control him or her, when a person becomes so ingrown and self-pitying that he or she refuses comfort, cannot reach out to others, and does not strive for growth.

Shock, denial, guilt, anger, restlessness or inactivity are all normal grief reactions. They become harmful only when they continue for an extended period of time, when it is evident that no progress has been made nor is intended.

What are some harmful grief characteristics?

Avoiding reality.

Doctors frequently prescribe sleeping pills for those first nights of grief. When pain sets in (which it will), how easy it is to mask that pain with drugs or with alcohol. Masking pain with drugs or alcohol is dangerous: a high percentage of widows become alcoholics. Loss of a loved one is painful, but handling these days with no "aids" is in the long run the healthiest, shortest route through the pain.

One must face reality and go through that pain—now or later—in order to heal. "You have to hurt if you are going to heal."

I am reminded of an elderly lady who knew how to face reality. Several years ago Emmett received a call from her asking him to visit. When he arrived, Anna told Emmett he could go in and talk with John, "but John has been very quiet today. He's just been sitting there."

Emmett went in to visit and realized that John was dead. When he told Anna, Anna ran to the phone and called her neighbor. "Hilda! John's been sitting here and he's deader than a doornail!" She immediately called the funeral director with the same message.

We try to stay away from the term "dead." Our denial? It is so much easier to say, "He passed away," "The Lord took him," "He's with the Lord." "Dead" seems so impersonal. But using the term is *facing reality.*

Our age has taught denial, but our grandparents faced death and the reality of loss. Anna faced reality! Facing death was a part of life.

Hanging on to the loved one's possessions or leaving his or her room and clothing untouched are other forms of not facing reality. Often this happens with the death of a child. It is one way of preserving the loved one and not facing reality.

Some persons turn away family and friends. Whether or not this is avoiding reality, I am not sure. It may be. Could these people be too painful a reminder of the loved one? Or has self-pity become so intense that families and friends are being refused?

Self-pity is an insidious feeling that can dominate a grieving person. Don't we all wallow in it at times? "I'm feeling sorry for me and I can do it better than anyone else. Just watch!"

Self-pity is evident when a grieving person continually says, "I'm not up to it." Granted, that is legitimate at first. But when does one become "up to it"? Self-pity cannot be used continuously as an excuse to allow one to wallow in his or her grief.

Repressing emotions. This elicits the "isn't he or she taking it well!" response. One thinks to oneself, "Be sure you don't break down in front of others." We all have stories to tell of those who seemingly did so well during those first days until after the funeral and then fell apart at the seams.

Being female has its advantages. We dare cry. There has been research done on tears. "William H. Frew II, a biochemist with the department of psychiatry at St. Paul-Ramsey Medical Center in Minnesota, believes that shedding tears rids the body of toxic chemicals produced under emotional stress. (His subjects alternately watched tearjerker movies like 'Brian's Song' and hovered over chopped onions.) Although it is too early for conclusive results, comparison of the tears shed in emotion and in response to eye irritants suggests that emotional tears do contain chemicals known to be associated with emotional stress."[4]

Men are daring more and more to weep openly today. That's

good. Society has placed on men a burden too great with the "big boys don't cry" syndrome.

The morning of Lin's funeral I found the most fantastic verse. I had remembered Lin sitting in the pulpit (toward the end of his illness, Lin had to sit to preach) lifting his hand up and saying, "God's hand is holding me!" I found and read Psalm 63:8:

> then I humbly follow thee with all my heart,
> and thy right hand is my support.

I called our assistant pastor, Lee Eliason, who would be leading the funeral service that day and shared what had just happened. I mentioned that during the sharing time scheduled in the funeral, if I felt up to it, I might say something.

Now, I wasn't consciously trying to be brave, but I believe I subconsciously may have been, because during the service I kept wondering if I should say something. So it appeared to others that I was very *brave*, except for those times when the songs of the service got to me. People said, "My, how she held up. How brave."

I did stand up and share that Scripture at the funeral. I am glad I did. It meant something to me later. Except I've wondered if it might have been better to give vent to my feelings at that "acceptable" time rather than repress them.

In June of that year our Conference, at its annual meeting, held a memorial service. Such a service is held every year in memory of those pastors and missionaries who have died. Their names are read and statistics given.

I was visiting a friend of mine nearby. She came with me. Emmett Johnson was there and offered to sit with us during the memorial service.

That year they sang for the first time Lin's and my favorite song, "For All the Saints." I was going to record this service. However, as soon as they began singing, I began sobbing. All that is heard on my recording are gulping sobs—over and over and over. I leaned into Emmett's shoulder. He kept saying, "You're going to make it." He tried desperately to reassure and comfort me, all to no avail. There we were, close to the front and right in the middle, where it was all but impossible to leave.

I wonder if it would have been better to have cried more at the funeral. Was this pent-up emotion that had to be released? I don't know. Suppressed emotions have to come out sometime.

There is nothing noble in suppressing emotions, whatever they may be. As a friend said, "Tears let the hurt out."

There are those who seemingly do not have a sense of loss. They go on as before, never mentioning the person they have lost. They shed no tears. "Isn't she holding up?" No! There *is* a loss. It has to be admitted and faced squarely.

Loss can be expressed in hyperactivity, getting into work so much that one becomes a "workaholic," coming home exhausted so that all there is left to do is crawl into bed. "Put it out of your mind, maybe it will go away."

Some try to become what their partner was—active church member, business-person. They attempt to take over where the loved one left off.

Harmful grief.

There is pain in the process of grief. However, there can be growth in grief and growth through pain.

People have to be willing to grow; they have to be willing to accept pain. It takes time. It takes work.

Grief work has been defined as "reviewing the life of the one who died, going back over it, remembering it, then burying these things, recognizing their finality."[5]

Going through possessions and clothing can be the best thing for this grief work. Remembering all those good times, those good memories—reviewing that life, then burying it.

Pictures help. Going over them, realizing the person is gone, recognizing the finality, and burying that life.

I think writing my first book helped. I had to listen to Lin's voice, to his sermons. Sometimes the hurt seemed unbearable, but I believe it helped in the healing process. I heard that voice, but I realized he was no longer there, that he was not coming back. He was dead and buried.

Facing pain squarely is better than masking or avoiding it.

In managing grief, Edgar Jackson says there are at least three important steps:

The first step is that "of facing the full reality of what has happened." He mentions, as I have, resisting detours—alcohol, drugs. "We need courage to endure the pain, aware that ours is essentially a healthy pain. It is one that has within it its own healing qualities."

The second step is "breaking some of the bonds that tie us to the person who has died . . . withdrawing the emotional capital from the past so that our feelings can be reinvested in the future."[6]

A wife can be very dependent on her husband. It was easy to go on saying, "What would Lin do?" That tie had to be broken. Lin was no longer there. I had to reinvest in the future.

The third step is "to develop ways that will make it possible for the person to find new interests, satisfactions and creative activities for the remainder of his life. New relationships must be formed, new acquaintances made."[7]

Face the reality, break bonds, reinvest in the future, and develop new interests and goals.

"There is no easy way to accept death [or divorce]. We each must find our own process. We may be helped by good memories, by time, and by expressing our feelings. When our acceptance is coupled with self-affirmation, we have made a great stride."[8]

Hard times will be there, depression will come, but the storm will subside and the sun will shine again.

After Good Friday . . . Resurrection!

The Final Good-Bye

We see ads in newspapers and in magazines for funeral homes and for cemeteries. People call on the phone regarding cemetery lots and the caller is shocked if you already have purchased a cemetery lot.

We may see the ads, but we pass over them. Not often does one say, "What a fine ad for a vault. I think I'll read this carefully."

We don't read them.

We don't talk about death.

We want life. And life is good.

Our use of language shows us how we deny death: "passed away," "gone to be with the Lord." Even in the past, the room where the body was laid was called a "slumber room." I went through a local cemetery the other day. The entrance road to the cemetery, the burial place for the *dead*, was called "Slumber Lane."

Our grandparents and those before them could not deny death in the same way that we can today. People died at home; they were "laid out" at home; and they were buried from home, usually in a family plot or a community cemetery. Children knew very well when Mother or Grandma was preparing the body. They would be in the home and around the body for the few days before burial.

In the past, emotions were expressed more openly. Some cultures had regular rituals where there would be moaning and wailing over the body of the dead. Days were set aside for this before burial took place. Not so today. Our funeral homes and hospitals take the place of the home and sometimes of the family. Often the family is not even present when a loved one dies.

It is important to consider the preparations, the reviewal, the

funeral director, and the funeral itself. (The reviewal is sometimes called a viewing, a wake, and other terms. I will be calling
it a reviewal. It was that for me—a reviewing of memories,
reviewing our life together, not just viewing a body.)

Questions frequently arise as to when a funeral should be
planned. Before answering that question, I would like to discuss
other pertinent NOW preparations: the pre-funeral, pre-illness
preparations that pass us by no matter how young or old we
may be.

Most younger people do not have wills. We do not think
about wills when we are young. "It's not necessary right now,
you see."

We were planning a will the day Lin died. It was never finished.

A will should be made. Laws vary from state to state. People
want to have some say in how their families are cared for. A
will, at a nominal cost, provides this.

Along with the will, an executor of your estate should be
chosen, a trusted friend or adviser. Incidentally, the executor
sometimes must be from the state where you reside. Check laws
in your state about the matters that concern you.

What about your financial situation at home? Do both spouses
know about the finances in the home? Do you both know about
bills, investments, property, your business? Are you aware of
what is going on? This needs to be considered *now*.

In the past, financial matters in the home were usually the
husband's responsibility. Yet many men died before women. So
we have many "poor" widows left at the mercy of relatives and
friends. Sometimes there are unscrupulous lawyers or relatives
who take advantage of the survivor.

You and your spouse and loved ones should be aware of
insurance policies and retirement programs, along with other
pertinent information concerning safe deposit box, cemetery lot,
social security number, banks, veteran's benefits. This should
all be kept available in one place.*

If you are anything like I am, you keep putting those things
off, thinking "someday, when I get older, I'll plan some of those
things." "Older" for me was age 34.

The Preparation

When should I plan a funeral?

*See Appendix—"Information for Survivors"

After a particularly difficult time when my husband was in the hospital, he wrote,

> I am being faced with death again. I certainly did not invite this intrusion. There is so much I would like to do—so many exciting things in life. But I have no real choice in the matter.
>
> The tests and treatment seem to get worse as we go along. The spinal taps and injections were terrible, but I made it. I hate this double vision. I look a mess—no hair and one eye covered. But I will fight this thing with the strength of God. I still feel He has much for me to do. I am assured of a great God who comes to me in such times.[1]

During that time, I, too, had to face death, the reality that my husband might die. I battled that with God, with tears, and with God's Word. Two days later I was more at peace and had an extraordinary experience that I recorded.

> Instead of reading Scripture . . . I went through the hymnal, picking out hymns of praise and singing and singing. "For All the Saints" was the hymn that stood out to me. I called Lin in the morning and read the words to him over the phone. And later that day in the hospital, we sang the hymn together, with tears streaming down our faces. . . .
>
> I decided that "For All the Saints" just had to be sung. Maybe the choir could sing "To God Be the Glory." Someone would have to sing "Complete in Thee," and perhaps "He Giveth More Grace."
>
> And since "Sharing Time" had become such an important part of the life of the church, especially on Sunday nights, I knew Lin would like a sharing time at his final service. Having thought it through, I put the plans aside. I would bring them out sooner than I dreamed.[2]

It was good for me to be able to plan the funeral ahead of time.

I advocate that procedure for several reasons.

First, there isn't the pressure of "this will be the last thing I can do for my loved one, I'd better make it good (costly!)."

The "good" happens when the cost isn't considered as much as having a meaningful service for those in attendance, and one that your loved one would want.

Second, the two of you can discuss what you want accomplished at the service. You can discuss possible pallbearers, favorite songs, the minister you would prefer, organist, soloist, favorite Scriptures. Even if it isn't planned, I guess you can see the value in such a discussion. It is important for those closest to us to have a part in planning. I'm glad we did.

Third, it brings the subject of death out in the open and gives each one the opportunity to share his or her thoughts and wishes. You can deal with death, its reality, and then go on with life so that when it comes time to die, all you have left to do is to die.

In a class discussion one member commented: "I think it is a wonderful idea (to plan the funeral ahead). My mother planned hers. She even planned what dress she would wear, what jewelry she should wear, what music should be played, everything. And it was *so* beautiful. And there wasn't any hassle. My brothers and sisters and I have different religious convictions—all Christians, but very different ideas. Consequently there would have been some problems and differences of opinions. My father would have had to settle the arrangements and arbitrate the disagreements. This way, she had it just the way she wanted it."

"I have always felt that the funeral service should be a celebration," said another member of that class. "It wouldn't be so bad to have 'When the Saints Go Marching In' sung at the funeral."

Joyce Landorf, author, lecturer and singer, was speaking at a conference I attended. She told about her family discussing funerals. As with many serious discussions, they became silly. Her husband said what he wanted was a life-size portrait above his casket with his hand extended as in a handshake, and a recording saying, "So glad you could come!" She said she could just see herself and the children at his funeral snickering, thinking about their conversation.

Preparing ahead of time helps one face death and get on with life.

During our class, the subject of cremation came up.

"A friend of mine had asked me to bury him at sea," said a class member. "He was an avid fisherman. He was cremated and I kept his ashes in a bottle in the basement. I thought that would be the logical place to keep them.

"I was going on a fishing trip and took the bottle with me. I didn't want to spoil the fishing for the rest of them, so I had an agreement with the captain that at the end of the day, before heading back, we would say a few words and sprinkle my friend's ashes on the sea. Just before heading back, we told the men what we would be doing. As I began saying a few words, I looked around, and all those fishermen had their hats off and placed at their hearts in honor of a fellow fisherman. It was a moving experience."

The Reviewal

I recall people telling me years ago that they did not want an open casket at a "wake." "It is so *pagan!*"

Let me share with you my experience.

I was with my husband when he died in the hospital. I remember to this day that last breath. I watched him fall into unconsciousness and, one and a half hours later, die. He struggled. He wanted to live. Or, in that struggle, was he saying, "I'm ready to go"? I don't know. I wanted him to live. He died. I saw him die. Yet it seemed so unreal.

When I saw his body at the funeral home, I could see that that was what had housed Lin. Lin was gone. I needed to see that. My family needed to see the body, my boys needed to. Reality came sooner for me because of viewing the body of my husband. Rather than being "pagan," it was helping me face reality.

Several years before that day, a dear friend of mine, Bob Samuelson, had died. In fact, our middle son was named after him. Bob and his brother, John, and I had been together for a long time; we were about the only ones in our youth group. Bob died quite suddenly. He was a vivacious person, always up to something, always having a good time. I wanted to remember Bob that way. So I didn't view the body.

I had more dreams about Bob (like seeing him running to do something, but being dead—unreal dreams) than I had about my own husband after he died.

Bob's death didn't become settled for me. Reality was a long time in coming. I could not really remember Bob as he was. How much better to have had it settled sooner.

At Lin's reviewal I was able to talk to people. People came to see *me*, not only to give respect to Lin. They talked with me, more so than after the funeral. I cried with many that day. I even laughed with some.

I remember a friend whom I hadn't seen in several years coming into the funeral home. Her hair was a mess! My sister leaned over to me and said, "We'll have to get the name of her hairdresser!" We burst into laughter. People may have questioned that laughter, but it eased the tension and the despair of the moment.

At the reviewal I was able to spend time in reflection going back over memories and our life together.

William Donald II, in his pamphlet entitled "The Therapy of Grief," talks about the reviewal. "It is the result of the psychological need for sharing grief. The Irish wake has its roots in Jewish tradition which dates back at least to Old Testament days. The people came and reminisced about the deceased. They gave each other of their devotion and affection. They sustained their loss mutually."[3]

Every culture has its rites, traditions, and ceremonies for burying the dead. The body has been important in life. We can accord it dignity in death. This is illustrated by the New Testament example of the woman who used rare and expensive ointment to prepare the body of Jesus for burial. A part of the grieving process for those remaining is to bring closure to a relationship that once was.

The time of reviewal was important for me, as was the funeral. At the reviewal I was able to talk with the people, cry with most, laugh with some. There was ministry taking place that day. And Lin looked dead. No matter how good the cosmetology was, Lin looked dead. I needed to see that.

Haven't you heard people say, "My, doesn't she look good? So natural."

Goodness, no!

I haven't seen a dead person look good, let alone natural, yet. Dead people look good compared to what they would look like if skilled hands had not prepared the body (aren't you glad for the practice of embalming and preservation?), but they do look dead, unnatural.

Preparing the body is important. Another aspect of this is mentioned by Charles Bauchmann:

> I'd like to believe that there would be family and friends who would accord me the dignity of a decent burial. Funerals, for me, emphasize the kind of identification I have tried to establish with other men, that they and I are persons of worth. If I say I believe in the Resurrection of the body, then why is this body suddenly so profane? I do not subscribe to the fact that this 'carcass' has no significance. Our Lord was accorded honor and dignity in His death. I don't know what kind of body I may have in the next world; this is the only one I have known, so please don't desecrate it by thinking that it is unimportant or not worthy of consideration.[4]

I like that.

Dr. Eric Lindemann, a leading authority on grief, speaks of

the importance of having a clear image of the dead person. A lack of such an image is one of the major causes of mental and emotional disturbances as a result of unwisely managed grief. He claims that these emotionally disturbed individuals cannot remember the image of the person who died. After the death of their loved one, they conveniently put the image of him or her out of their mind so as to avoid suffering. When they cannot bring the person to mind, it serves to keep the pain at a distance since grief is one of the post painful emotions that a person faces. Some do manage to avoid the pain, and too late they see how costly it was to their emotional and mental well-being, a great price to pay for temporary relief of pain. The loss to the bereaved needs to be felt fully. "You have to hurt if you are going to heal." To grasp the reality of the loss, one could stand beside the casket establishing the image of the person in one's mind. As feelings are faced and the finality of the loss takes place, reorganization of life begins.[5]

Consider the struggle of those who have lost their loved ones during the war and have no mental picture of them. For them, grief work takes an unusually long time.

My mother-in-law was in the hospital when her son and my husband died. A year and a half later she was commenting on how difficult it was still to try to listen to any of the sermons he had preached.

For some, the actual viewing of the body is offensive. When a friend of mine was asked if she wanted an open casket, the response was loud and clear, "No! I want it closed. Life is over." But I would comment that the reviewal and the funeral are for the bereaved, to aid them in their grieving process.

Grief cannot be programmed. Each has his or her feelings. If those feelings are strong, they should, if possible, be honored.

The reviewal, for me, definitely had a significant part in the healing of my grief.

The Funeral Director

The funeral director has had much publicity in the last few years, usually unfavorable.

My experience was a good one. I can only say good things about the treatment I received, the care and consideration for my feelings and my wishes. It was the funeral director who helped me purchase a cemetery lot the week before my husband died. I had been told Lin had two weeks at the most to live, maybe less. The day after being told that I contacted Emmett Johnson and told him the gravity of the situation. "I have the funeral planned, but I don't have any idea about a funeral director or a cemetery lot." Emmett contacted the funeral director he had known through his church, who was well respected and known in the Minneapolis-St. Paul area.

A funeral home that is used consistently by the church of which you are a member would be reliable or else the church would go to another.

The funeral director I used, Larry Osborne, was trusted and trustable. He knew all the ins and outs of planning a funeral— cards for thank-yous, what to do about honorariums for those officiating and helping with the service, motorcades, where to get a casket in an affordable price range, and the laws regarding vaults (low-cost vaults are very acceptable and are usually covered with green "grass-like" material). At times, especially during the winter, people are not present for the actual burial. The vault is often not at the grave site until long after the family leaves and the ground can be adequately prepared. An expensive vault would be an unnecessary extravagance.

The funeral director will help with the obituary for the local papers and the paper in the hometown of the deceased. It is in the obituary that you can designate memorials in lieu of flowers and where to have the memorials sent—to the church, the American Cancer Society, the Multiple Sclerosis Society, or any favorite charity. You can write the obituary yourself and give the information you would like to be known rather than what someone else considers necessary.

The funeral director was a great help even after the funeral. I had questions about social security and about some financial matters. He knew what to do and gave me the instructions I needed. Check with your church as to whom is recommended and visit him or her. Questions can be asked and you will receive the answers.

The Funeral Service

There is great value in the funeral service. There is a need for us to acknowledge the passing from this life to the next—a "rite" of passage. The funeral service provides this.

The funeral is for the living.

It is an acceptable time in which the feelings of grief can be openly displayed. It is a time in which friends and the community can come together to share their loss with the bereaved and with each other. It is a time for an expression of religious faith and in which those in attendance can offer support and encouragement to the bereaved. The funeral can offer hope in the midst of the reality of death.

Roy Pearson, in an article entitled "Let's Be Sensible About Funerals," said,

> The funeral service gives friends and relatives a chance to gather up in their minds the total life of the one who has gone, to hold that life in single memory, and to express their gratitude that the life was lived. . . . Still further, the funeral service is meant to bring consolation and hope to those who are bereaved, to deepen their sense of God's presence and care in this time of their loss, and to send them back to their daily work with faith and courage.[6]

For me the funeral was a celebration. The name of Christ was uplifted and hope was given to me, to my boys, and to the believers assembled there. That is the way it should be.

C. Charles Bachmann says, "The funeral serves to personalize and to actualize the loss." It is "a vehicle for the expression of grief."[7] What better place to express those deep feelings than at a service designed just for that. Edgar Johnson, in his book *You and Your Grief*, says of the funeral that it "reinforces the fact that death has taken place, and that your loved one is gone beyond recall."[8]

By losing your loved one by death, there is a final good-bye. In divorce, couples still see each other and this stretches the separation process. The "good-bye," the parting, is not permanent. In many divorces there is a grieving process and it takes longer. There is no burial, no funeral. Other means of grieving must take place—maybe a letter of release (not necessarily mailed) or talking before or after the divorce when the "reviewal" takes place and the emotions are "buried."

I recall knowing, intellectually, that Lin was not coming back, yet struggling with the feeling that he might. The reviewal and funeral helped me accept the reality that Lin would not return. And that helped me to go on with the painful but important task of living!

Seymour Shubin was one who never "bothered" attending funerals of others until the funeral of his father. He says,

> Before the service began we entered a room just off the chapel, and soon people began coming in. One of the first was an elderly man I didn't know. He held my hand for a moment as he said,

"You wouldn't remember me, but I worked for your Dad when he first started business. He was a real gentleman." Just that, and he was gone.

But inside, where there had been emptiness, I felt a strange glow. And it grew, this glow, as the line inched by. . . .

Now others were approaching, friends who, though their words might be awkward or mumbled, brought the priceless gift of themselves. How grateful I was for their presence; how infrequently I had given mine. . . .

Recently, the father of a dear friend of mine died, and although I had not known the father well, I made it my business to attend the funeral. Later my friend said to me, "It may sound strange to use the word happy, but there really was a kind of happiness in seeing you. It had nothing to do with being comforted; it was just that I was so glad you were there. I've been to many funerals," he went on, "but I never knew until now how important it was to go."

I nodded, remembering the solace of a deep and personal grief shared when I, too, had been in that first row.[9]

At the funeral of our friend, Paul Greely, the service brochure had a quotation from Paul when he had spoken at a chapel service: "Like I said, I don't believe that God is through with me yet, but if he is, I guess you could say I believe in tomorrow no matter what happens. I believe in tomorrow whether or not I am alive on this earth or in heaven with the Lord."

How to Help the Hurting

What to say, what to do, how to help someone who has lost a loved one have been questions asked forever. We struggle with what to say when someone dies. Often we don't say *anything* when someone is divorced. It is easier to say nothing.

Grief and bereavement are a part of losing a loved one through death or divorce. There is a loss even if a marriage was difficult and painful.

The words from Grandma Fiscus, "I'm praying that God will wrap cotton around your heart," were a constant source of comfort for me. "More cotton, Lord," was a frequent cry in those early stages of grief. I even pray that now when times are tougher than usual. "I need some cotton, Lord."

People are the most important gift during bereavement. We *can* all be of help even though constant and unanswered questions are pounding in on us.

We can send a card whether or not we know the family intimately. Cards say, "I care."

The card is important, but even more important is to *write* on the card. However, a verse not to include is Romans 8:28 (KJV), "We know that all things work together for good to them who love God. . . ." The bereaved may know that, but they do not need to hear that at this time. Initially they are struggling with the pain of grief, not trying to figure out how God is going to use this for good.

The God who created them is walking with them. They may not know the why, but God *is* there. Leslie Weatherhead included a moving example of God's presence in his book *Why Do Men Suffer?* "I think that thought of his, that 'not a sparrow falleth to the ground without your heavenly Father,' is one of

the tenderest in the New Testament. So moving is it that when
. . . I saw a dead sparrow on the grass of the great court at
Trinity College, Cambridge, I had a queer impulse to take it up
and bury it tenderly for the sake of the One who was with it
when it fell."[1] If God cares for the sparrow, how much greater
must he care for us, made in His image. He *is* with us when we
fall, when we suffer. There is no real *answer* to suffering, only
that God is there with us.

It is good to remember the bereaved person during special
events such as Christmas, Thanksgiving, Easter, family times—
Fourth of July, Memorial Day, Labor Day. These are often the
"sneaky" times when a look, a song, a comment brings back
the pain of bereavement. A card now and then with the words,
"I've been thinking of you," can help to ease those moments.

Verses of Scripture, if they have been meaningful to the writer,
are nice on cards. For instance, my favorite verse is Psalm 57:1,

> I will take refuge in the shadow of thy wings
> until the storms are past.

I write on the card that this verse has meant a lot to me and
maybe will mean something to the person to whom I'm writing.

I began reading the Psalms when someone wrote a reference
on a card and I looked it up. It meant something to me and I
began reading there.

The physical presence of friends is important. Be there. Listen.
Care. A friend can bring food or help clean the house and just
be there, available if the grieving person wants to talk.

If, when you are helping, you are asked why the tragedy has
occurred, don't feel you have to try to give an answer. To say,
"I don't know, it doesn't make any sense," may be sufficient.
The need to talk and have someone listen is the important thing,
not answers to profound questions.

God *has* been with us before; chances are, He'll be there again!
I may not see that now. All I see is the hiddenness of God. But
He is there and walks with us.

When Lin died, I needed a support system. The church was
there. There is comfort in numbers, in the feeling of being
included. It was also good to have one or two people at a time
minister to me in their own way.

My friend, Gordy Lindquist, didn't need to say anything to
me. At the funeral home he sat by the casket, weeping unas-
hamedly over the loss of his good friend. His wife, Joyce, said

later, "I think his loss was almost as great as yours." That said
to me, "We care."

Scripture says to weep with those who weep. William Hulme,
professor, author, and lecturer, said, "We want to make them
feel better so we don't weep and they don't weep." Nobody
feels better! Burdens shared are lighter.

When William Hulme's daughter died, there were some he
expected to visit who did not come. The reason? "We thought
you wanted to be alone. We thought you would have plenty of
others. We did not want to intrude or interfere." Yet it is very
hard for the bereaved to take the initiative. We need people.
We need their presence, their touch. Let the bereaved decide
that they do not need you! If you are friends, assume they do
want and need you.

Friends can help by sharing of themselves, by honestly expressing their feelings. You can say, for instance, "I am feeling
so sorry." Or, "I don't know what to say. This makes no sense
to me. I cared for him/her, and I care for you. I want to stand
by to help. Will you help me know what I can do, how I can
help? This might help me in my grief also." That may help the
bereaved person to begin talking because you are putting yourself in a position where you are asking him or her to help you.

In being there, providing the ministry of presence, you can
go where that person takes you. Look for cues. You might say,
"You seem so tired today." Allow for a response. There is no
need to do all the talking. Being at the side of a friend may be
all that is needed.

A touch, a squeeze on the arm, a hug, is ever so important.
I missed the intimacy with my husband.

When I was working at Shoreview Treatment Center (for
alcoholics and drug users), I received hugs now and then. I
thought I was hugging. But actually our bodies formed a pyr-
amid. I would gently, oh, so gently, put my arms around the
shoulder of the hug-ee, with my feet at least a foot away from
the other person's feet! One time, as I returned a hug, the one
receiving my hug told me, "You know, that's the first time
you've really hugged." I didn't realize what a non-hugger I was!
A warm hug, a body hug, saying, "I'm here, I care," means
much and costs little.

We should go slow on giving advice. Advice often borders on
arrogance.

I received letters from one well-meaning widow who peppered the letters with, "Now, one word of advice." At that moment I felt like screaming, "I don't need advice. I need someone who cares!"

My son, Steve, when he was 14, was asked by a friend to be with him at the reviewal and the funeral of his friend's mother who had been killed. I asked Steve what he said. "Nothing. I was just with him." Another friend lost his brother in a motorcycle accident. Again, this friend asked Steve to be with him during those hours at the mortuary. He knew Steve had been where he was. He needed someone who understood to stand by and to care. Friends are needed. They were God's gift to me.

Wednesday, November 21, 1973. Tonight was the Thanksgiving service and I babysat in the nursery. After the service, people gave beautiful expressions of love. Lynnell, one of the young people, came up to me and said, "Thank you for being a member of our church and I appreciate so much your being our Sunday school teacher." Then Dick Turnwall came up and said, "I just want to let you know that we do love you." Lee (associate pastor when Lin lived, now interim pastor) came up and said the same thing. It was a service that I'm glad I missed because I think it would have been too hard for me. I'm glad that even though I wasn't in the service I could be a part of it by having people come up to me and give me expressions of love.

An expression of love for me was being invited into homes of couples and feeling included. The newly single may not be eager to accept invitations, however. A comfortable, nonthreatening coffee, dinner, or party with close friends present could ease the single into a social life again. Many newly single persons are not comfortable with couples for a long time, but they should continue to be invited. That first step is an extremely precarious step. The sooner it is taken, the better. You could help make that first step less painful.

It meant much to me to be asked to dinner with two couples the Saturday after Lin's funeral. Even if I had not gone, the gesture was meaningful. But I did go. I had a difficult time, but the next time was much easier and the time after, easier yet, until one day I was very comfortable in any situation. I had to take that first step. Those two couples helped me make that step.

The entire family could be invited into your home. All need the feeling of being remembered. The children need to see other families in operation. Modeling helps their development. At home these children live in a one-parent family day after day after day. If children are invited to homes frequently where mother and father are working with their children, it will give them role models.

Singles could also invite others into their homes. By inviting couples into your home, you are showing them you are comfortable with them. Chances are, the single family will be included more often.

Churches need to minister to the entire family. Two-thirds of church members are singles and single-parent families. Check the scheduling and the class structures in your church and church schools. See if they are ministering to those families who do not have both parents in the home. We all need to try to break the patterns that exclude those who have the greatest needs, those who hurt the most.

The church family is one excellent way to help children of single-parent families feel included in family settings. Sunday school picnics are nonthreatening! These children can also be included in family outings and social events. Prayer-partners can be an adult matched with a child or youth. Classes can be taught by couples or a man-and-woman team.

The children from single-parent families face peculiar problems and struggles. When children know adults care, they are more apt to return that care and become caring people in our society. I John 4:19 (KJV) tells us: "We love him, because he first loved us." Love breeds love.

Practical things speak loudly of love and caring. Helping with car repairs, checking on the maintenance of furnace and plumbing, inviting a widow or widower to dinner, even suggesting how to sort clothes and use a washer, dryer, and dishwasher!

Because I was a pastor's wife, we had to do something I do not recommend as an added adjustment—move! Fortunately we moved only about a mile away, but it was still a big operation.

Wednesday, September 5, 1973. Whew, I'm beat. . . . Monday I moved! In *two hours* 2183 Mounds Avenue was empty and 5185 Bona Road was full. There must have been thirty people who showed up this Labor Day to help me! Couldn't believe it. My uncle came over with his trailer so we could use it. He came in to tell us it was there and when he got back outside, it was full—so he had to take a load over to the new house!

This is practical Christianity! People helping people. Yet, for me it was hard to accept help at times. Perhaps it was an admission to others that I had needs. I had to learn to admit that I had needs and that I needed help.

Sometimes, all people could offer me were clichés: "I know how you feel." No. They couldn't know. Yet they may have been people who did not know what to say or what to do, but they tried and that was o.k.

Advice was harder to take, especially from people who had never experienced what I was now experiencing.

Advice on medical treatment for those dying, or to the spouse, should *not* be given unless asked for. We had calls and letters suggesting diets, laetrile, and going to special faith healers. Our emotions were close to the surface anyhow. To compound this trauma by giving unasked-for advice is harmful. We felt that the medical services we were receiving represented the best medical help available. We had to rely on our doctors and to trust them. If we didn't, we would have sought help elsewhere.

One well-meaning person said to Emmett when his wife was dying, "If it were *my* wife, I'd spare no expense." The man didn't understand the hospital, the doctors, but most of all, he did not understand Darlene's wishes. She had a warm, loving staff, the most pleasant rooms in any hospital I have seen, good care, and she wanted to be there!

We all tend to be good advice-givers. If we don't know what to say, we give advice. Maybe a good rule to follow is simply to try to put yourself in the other person's place. Is it something *you* would like to hear?

Basically, people are caring. I received hundreds of cards. I was grateful for each person who took time to write, to call, to visit.

Philippians 4:14 says, "But it was kind of you to share the burden of my troubles." That's what I needed—someone to share my heavy load. The load was still there, but it was lighter because others shared it with me.

Me . . . Help Myself?

I have called the Bible my "Me Book." It tells me about me. Bob Benson, in his book, *Come Share the Being*, gave me that title. He has a "Winnie-the-Pooh" illustration I especially like.

A. A. Milne wrote the stories or told them first to his son, Christopher Robin. It begins with Christopher Robin coming down the stairs with his stuffed bear.

Here is Edward Bear, coming downstairs now, bump, bump, bump, on the back of his head behind Christopher Robin. It is, as far as he knows, the only way of coming downstairs, but sometimes he feels that there really must be another way, if only he could stop bumping and think of it. And then he feels that perhaps there isn't. Anyway, here he is at the bottom, and ready to be introduced to you. Winnie-the-Pooh. . . . "What about a story?" said Christopher Robin. "What about a story," I said. "Could you very sweetly tell Winnie-the-Pooh one?" "I suppose I could," I said. "What kind of stories does he like?" "About himself. Because he's that sort of bear."

And I suspect we are all *that* sort of bear. We like stories about ourselves. And this living book of God is about us. . . . We are in that book—it is a "me-book" and a "you-book." . . . These things were said to us and for us and about us in this living book of God. . . .

> We should be able to hear God
> smiling and breathing,
>   and whispering
> and shouting and laughing
>   and crying to us
>   in His word.[1]

I know that whenever I needed God, He was there. During those horrible times, as I read, God was there. So was I. The night before Lin died, I read Psalm 68:5. Be joyful and exult before him, "father of the fatherless, the widow's protector." I wrote alongside that verse, "I hope this isn't prophetic." The next night Lin died. But I knew where to turn.

The next chapter (Psalm 69:1-3) was me all over again.

Save me, O God;
for the waters have risen up to my neck.
I sink in muddy depths and have no foothold;
I am swept into deep water, and the flood carries me away.
I am wearied with crying out, my throat is sore,
my eyes grow dim as I wait for God to help me.

I felt I was sinking. I was being carried away. My throat was sore and I couldn't see for the tears! And I waited for God to help me. I did not receive a fantastic answer to prayer that night. But *I* was in God's word and that was what I needed to know at that time.

Later, when I was struggling over the "why" of Lin's death, it didn't make sense that a gifted preacher-pastor should be taken. I read Psalm 73:16, "So I set myself to think this out, but I found it too hard for me, until I went into God's sacred courts." "I need God's sacred courts more than my reasoning," I wrote next to that verse.

Psalm 77:1-6; 11-23 is especially dear. It describes the ups and downs I faced.

I cried aloud to God,
I cried to God, and he heard me.
In the day of my distress I sought the Lord,
and by night I lifted my outspread hands in prayer.
I lay sweating and nothing would cool me;
I refused all comfort.
[I did, too, at times!]
When I called God to mind, I groaned;
as I lay thinking, darkness came over my spirit.
My eyelids were tightly closed;
I was dazed and I could not speak.
My thoughts went back to times long past
[easy to do and okay if you don't dwell on the past!]
    I remembered forgotten years;
all night long I was in deep distress,
as I lay thinking, my spirit was sunk in despair.

But then, O LORD, I call to mind thy deeds;
I recall thy wonderful acts in times gone by
[and He had helped so much so often].
    I meditate upon thy works
    and muse on all that thou hast done.
O God, thy way is holy;
what god is so great as our God?

I have discovered David

[or Nancy, or Steve, Rob, or Scott]
my servant;
   I have anointed him with my holy oil.
My hand shall be ready to help him
   and my arm to give him strength."
                                    Psalm 89:20-21

The Lord, my rock, in whom there is no unrighteousness.
                                    Psalm 92:15

Alongside this last verse I wrote, "I may not have the answer to the why but this is sure—there is no unrighteousness in Him."

So God spoke—continues to speak—not audibly but through the Book, to my needs. God is in His Word, but during this time of grief I needed to know that I was there, too. The Bible is my "Me-Book" because it tells me about me.

When I think of God and His Word, prayer naturally comes to mind. Often, people ask, "Why pray?"

I don't know. It certainly isn't because God *needs* to hear from me.

But, *I need* to tell Him. I may even need to tell Him that I am angry, that my situation doesn't make sense.

My God is a big God and can handle those outbursts from His child. He remains constant.

He seems distant at times. My prayers don't seem to reach Him. Then, one day there He is again. And I learn that He never left. I did. In my anger, in my grief that was so unbearable, I left for a time.

He stayed.

Thy true love is firm as the ancient earth,
   thy faithfulness fixed as the heavens. (Psalm 89:2)

I remember being asked to lead a retreat on the subject of prayer. Emmett gave me an outline, and I've since heard his sermon on the subject. I like it.

There are three ways that God answers prayer.

First, He sometimes answers prayer all on His own—now or later, but He does it. Like the salvation of a loved one, or maybe even his or her physical healing. I wanted physical healing for Lin but it didn't happen. Luke 4:25-27 has helped me here. There were many widows in Zarepeta, but only to *one* was Elijah sent. Many lepers were in Jerusalem but only Namaan was healed. God does intervene. He heals, but it is the exception rather than the rule.

Second, God sometimes asks you to help. In fact, ninety percent of the time, prayer is answered with our help. As we pray, we will probably be asked to help with the answer. God says, "I'm so glad you asked about that. Now here is what I would like you to do. . . ."

Third, God may say, "I'll leave the situation as it is." In 2 Corinthians 12, Paul prayed three times to have the thorn in his flesh removed. God said, "We'll leave it as it is."

"But I'll change you." "My grace is sufficient for you for my power is made perfect in weakness" (2 Corinthians 12:9). It is. God's grace is there.

Lin wasn't healed. I was changed.

In a recent class one member said, "We need to pray more than God needs us to pray because we firm up in our minds what we believe, what our needs are, and what our faith is."

Another said, "Jesus didn't go to God in the Garden of Gethsemane and say, 'God, you know I don't want to die. Now You figure this thing out. You work it.' He said, 'Your will be done.'"

I thought about that. Jesus did say, "Your will be done," but only after he struggled so much that He actually sweat drops of blood, saying, "Let this cup pass from me. . . ." Maybe, just maybe, Jesus finally *knew* God's will. When the answer is known and God's will is known, I can say, "I see it, Lord! Thy will be done."

I prayed, "Lord, heal Lin. This is what I want. I'll leave You to work out the details of Your will." I didn't want to tell God what to do, but I did need to tell Him how I felt. That communication—prayer—was very important to me.

God's people were there. I don't know what I would have done without the people of God ministering to me, and encouraging me—unbeliever and believer alike.

When Emmett Johnson was sick, he had a Jewish oncologist, an agnostic radiologist, and an atheist, all working together to bring about the healing process in his life.

My dear neighbor, Sylvia, listened to more troubles and cried with me more than anyone. She gave me emotional and spiritual support. She cared.

People were there. Encouraging. Listening, Caring.

My friend, Alvera Mickelsen, kept encouraging me to write. "You write. I'll help make it interesting." And we wrote a book!

Emmett encouraged me to attend functions for pastors and

wives. What would I feel like that first time? All alone. I went. It was hard, but mostly it was affirming and what I needed at that time. I was able to talk with pastors again. I missed that. I could talk with both husbands and wives, sharing concerns that had been so familiar to me.

There are singles' organizations which the formerly-married single person can take advantage of for mutual help and encouragement. Singles can get together and begin their own interest groups, Bible studies, or family outings.

I served on a board for interviewing candidates for ordination, the Ministerial Guidance Committee. Was *that* a thrill. I read the doctrinal statements, reviewed and questioned the candidates and felt useful to the kingdom, not to mention feeling good about me. I was doing something for others.

A widow friend served her church by volunteering for an exciting ministry. Weekly she telephoned people who visited the church. She made many new friends and the church gained members.

People ministering to people. I had God and God's people. Philippians 4:12-14 says, "I have been very thoroughly initiated into the human lot with all its ups and downs. . . . I have strength for anything through him who gives me power. But it was kind of you to share the burden of my troubles."

I needed God, His strength, and I needed God's people to share the burden of my troubles—and sometimes I needed to take the initiative.

That first Christmas I was feeling very much alone. All the couples were inviting other couples to their homes after church. I finally asked one of the couples if I could come along if they were having people over after church that evening. I dared do that because of their friendship, but many singles may not have that much nerve and they sit home, alone. The forgotten people.

Getting out with others and finding new interests and satisfactions was rewarding. I began playing racquetball regularly. Others I know have joined tennis clubs or golf leagues. Taking children to parks, museums, or art galleries increases your awareness and theirs and takes the emotional capital from the past and reinvests in the future.

My journal was important to me. I needed to write. When I couldn't talk out my problems or concerns, I could write them out.

I found that I wrote—and at times I still do—when I *needed* to write. In that journal I saw a progression—from hurting, through pain, to healing. Writing was therapeutic for me.

The July after Lin's death the boys and I took our tent trailer and went to Arizona to visit my sister. Do you know what men do when they see a woman alone struggling to set up a tent trailer? Nothing! Then on the way home, it was my sister and I with *eight* kids, ages eleven and under, in a station wagon and pulling a tent trailer. How people stared! While in Arizona, I wrote:

> July 13, 1973. Tonight I was missing Lin again as I saw Bruce playing with the boys, and seeing Steve and Rob and Scotty needing a daddy. I just had to pray again to ease my loneliness.
>
> Tonight I felt it was unfair that Lin had to be taken from me. The boys need a dad so much and I feel inadequate to be both.
>
> Then I thought of Lin's life. His childhood was full of suffering and sadness. And he *did* accomplish so much these past years. It seems as though God was saying, "Lin, you're ready now. You're almost what I want you to be. I'll only allow you to go through this terrible thing of cancer for a short time and then I'll bring you Home—to fullness and completeness with NO MORE PAIN TO BEAR. Your suffering is over. You've added your share in filling up what was lacking in the suffering of Christ. Now people will understand Me a bit better, too. Your loved ones will understand, too, so it's time to come.

And now heaven is just a little bit dearer to me because Lin is there.

Even though the pain was there, it helped to write out those feelings. And the *need* to write became less frequent.

Just as keeping my journal helped in the healing of grief, so writing my book helped.

I began by typing Lin's sermons on the Apostles' Creed. It meant listening to his voice that I would never hear in person again. I stopped many times because I was sobbing too hard to carry on. I'd cry out to God and plead with Him to "use this book because it hurts so much to write."

I began the book about a month after Lin's death. I do believe that because of reliving so much so deeply, healing was quite complete.

It does help, also, to know that you are helping others. I kept telling myself that because of my book someday, someone somewhere in a hard place would know there is hope and say, "I can make it."

Helping others helps the hurt seem worthwhile. When others saw that I had made it, it gave them enough to go on for a day, and the next day, and the day after that. It is like the Alcoholics Anonymous "Twelfth Step": helping another on the road to recovery.

I remember talking to a woman whose husband had died the month before. She was so torn apart that she said the only thing preventing her from committing suicide was that she had to care for her children, still very young. But after talking, she thanked me and said she knew she could make it because I had.

Helping her helped me. It got my mind off my pain. It set me on the path toward reality. I was alive. Life could be good again for me and for those I love.

God's love is unfailing. He gives life—life abundant—if I'm willing to accept it.

Then Came Problems

A lone Again, Naturally," a song once said. After being two, becoming one is not natural, no matter why one is alone.

For twelve years we were together, sharing thoughts and dreams, arguing over finances or the children. We had good times mostly, but some angry times as well.

Now I was alone. No longer could I go to my partner to ask a question regarding the Bible study I was leading. I could not share accomplishments that had taken place, dreams nor the difficult times I was having. I had to do it alone.

The song, "Jesus Walked This Lonesome Valley," often came to mind.

> Jesus walked this lonesome valley,
> He had to walk it by Himself;
> O nobody else could walk it for Him,
> He had to walk it by Himself.
>
> As we walk our lonesome valley,
> We do not walk it by ourselves;
> For God sent His Son to walk it with us,
> We do not walk it by ourselves.[1]

We have Christ, I knew that. But I also felt I needed Christ *embodied* and I needed my closest friend, my companion, my lover.

Being alone, I now needed to learn how to do the typical "male-type" things around the house. Plumbing, heating, car maintenance, yard work, house repair. Some jobs I had done, some were foreign to me.

I remember the first time I tried fixing a faucet. It was leaking just a little. I thought, "Well, this is just a little loose so I'm going to tighten it." I had a pipe wrench. "If I just loosen this a tad and wipe off the washer some. . . ." All of a sudden there was water spurting everywhere, shooting up into the air, splashing me and the floor. I felt like Lucille Ball. And I had no idea where to turn off the water. I tried stuffing a wash cloth in the gaping hole; it didn't work!

Finally, I got the water shut off and called my neighbor to come and help. We found parts of that faucet all over the flooded kitchen. My neighbor, Bill, fixed it.

It was hard to realize that I would not be receiving help now unless I asked someone for it. I no longer had built-in help that I had taken for granted.

Men have similar problems. They must take over "female" tasks. Socks and underwear turn tattletale gray. Phil Donahue recounted his experiences in the *Philadelphia Inquirer* on April 1, 1980. "For a while I was convinced that parenthood equaled socks. I couldn't believe how many there were, and how dirty they looked. Not just tattletale gray—they were black. In fact, I was beginning to notice a lot of things that had never caught my attention before—like other people's floors. Without knowing it, I was slowly being absorbed into a whole new life experience. It is called motherhood.

"At the laundromat, I would be caught with two full washing machines and no change, staggered by the number of coin boxes and coin combinations that they took. And I had to hover as the spin cycle ended for fear that an angry fellow customer would empty my machine with less concern for the contents than I had. And all the while I was trying to look comfortable (and praying that I would not be recognized) by trying to read an old magazine in the glare of fluorescent light. . . . And I soon became a very sophisticated domestic; the Downy goes in the rinse cycle."[2]

Facing the fact that I was alone had its ups and downs. Philip W. Williams recounts a session with Wilma, one of his counselees. "After the death of her husband, Wilma felt like a clock's pendulum. Her emotions moved from one side to the other." Wilma said, "I don't like having to do everything he used to do. Before you knew it though, I learned how to do the things he used to do, and I even liked some of that responsibility. In fact, my independence lets me do as I will.

"I'm probably going to get a job like I wanted. When Bert was alive, he didn't want me to work. You see, one minute I want to be dependent and the next minute I like my independence."[3]

I was alone now and quite independent.

We took a trip to Phoenix at Christmas. I decided that the best way, with three children, was to go by Amtrak. I am now not good advertising for Amtrak.

In September I made reservations. When I make reservations with an airline company, I arrive and there is a seat. Not so on Amtrak.

We arrived at the station early—6 A.M. This gave us ample time before the train was scheduled to leave. The train was to be late so we were told *not* to check our baggage. I was there with ten bags and three small boys and we were to carry the luggage!

To get to Phoenix from Minneapolis is a challenge. You go via Chicago and from there to Flagstaff where you must be met.

At the Amtrak station we waited. And waited . . . and waited. Four hours. Every twenty minutes, they announced a delay.

We finally arrived in Chicago—half an hour after our connecting train had left! At least eighty of us were stranded in Chicago.

Amtrak put us up in the elegant Palmer House. We were in jeans to be comfortable for travel. Three kids and jeans.

We were hungry. The coffee shop at the Palmer House was closed for remodeling. So there we were: three grubby kids and one adult eating fancy French food in the Palmer House restaurant, courtesy of Amtrak.

The next day—our fault, not Amtrak's—we were almost late again. We had visited some friends in Chicago (that had been a bonus), but we were caught in a traffic jam on the way to the station. There was no time to check the luggage. We staggered on the train again with our ten bags.

Shortly after we left Chicago for Arizona we ran into a blizzard. It was thirty-six hours before we arrived in Flagstaff. When I woke Scott (age three) at four o'clock in the morning, he rubbed his eyes and said, "Do we hasta run to anudder train?"

On the trip home the train was late again. This time Amtrak put us in the Holiday Inn. I had to be aggressive there. Taxi drivers do *not* like taking one woman, three boys, and ten pieces of luggage. I finally had to open the door of a cab, get in, and tell the driver where we were going.

I smiled when I realized that if Lin were alive, I would probably be saying—loudly—"Why did you do this? Why did you choose this way to go?" I preferred to blame somebody. Now there was no one to blame except myself.

Wanting to be independent and liking it, yet needing the comfort of dependence at times, was like being a yo-yo. Up and down.

I needed to learn to accept my aloneness. I found I needed solitude—a place to go to cry, to be alone with my thoughts and my struggles and work them through. My bedroom became that place. I went there (and still do) to think, pray, holler if I have to, and to work through difficult times. I treasured those times of being alone—just me and God. I still need them. They are learning and growing times.

I suppose I was going through an identity crisis. Twelve years before Lin's death when we were married, I never gave my identity a thought. Seven of those twelve years I had been a pastor's wife. I loved being a pastor's wife. I loved the people, and I think they loved me. It was hard for me to get myself *out* of the role of being a pastor's wife.

One minister told my parents to encourage me to leave the church and the area. "It would be best." It was bad advice. I recently read that the best place to face readjustment is where the readjustment must finally be made. I found that to be true. I needed to stay. I needed to readjust in that place where Lin had died, where all my friends were, and where the people of God were at hand to support me. I had to change from being a pastor's wife to being a regular member of the congregation.

A major change for me was purchasing my own home and moving out of the parsonage. For me this move solidified the fact that I was no longer the pastor's wife whose housing needs would be cared for. With that purchase, I quickly learned to be independent. The excitement of buying and decorating a new home made the transition easier.

I was withdrawing from the role of pastor's wife when the church called a new pastor, Mike Halcomb. While he was candidating, it was not hard to listen to him preach. In fact, I had known him and his wife during seminary days, but when I saw him with his son who was the same age as Scott, the pain was intense.

The installation service was very difficult for me.

Sunday, October 28, 1973. This day has to take the prize for my hardest day in church! It was the Halcombs' first Sunday. Had he not had Communion, I think I could have coped. But there's too much *thinking* in Communion. It didn't seem right to have someone taking Lin's place when Lin had been such an excellent preacher! Emmett was going to speak in the evening service and the last time he spoke was at the funeral. Marilyn played "When He Shall Come," and that was as far as my composure could go.

The welcoming service was tonight and again I struggled, to no avail, to keep the tears back. Singing "Does Jesus Care?" was dreadful. Gordy Lindquist shared with me how he had struggled that day. Three others came to me and said similar things. Emmett and Lee were concerned as were others. So very many shared my hurt. But of course that made it even harder—with all these dear people. But I had to work through this day. I Peter's "smarting" sure means a lot tonight. Oh, am I smarting!

I had just begun to heal. Opening the old wounds was just too much. I needed more healing. Now I wasn't "giving up" being a pastor's wife. The role had been taken from me. I no longer had the choice.

The situation was resolved for me ten months later when the pastor and I were both teachers at a youth camp in Northern Minnesota. I was able to talk it all out and we came to understand each other better.

Identity. During our marriage I hadn't felt I had to "play a role" as a pastor's wife. I didn't feel as a pastor's wife I had to be anyone different from Nancy Karo. I enjoyed the things I did and would have done them anyway—pastor's wife or not.

I remember particularly an incident in a small rural church in which one lady was quite critical of the youth. Her criticism naturally affected aspects of her life and that of the church. We were at the church at a time when skirts were being raised close to the knee. I, being young and wanting to be stylish, hemmed some skirts to what I considered to be the proper stylish length. Sure enough, one day after church the critical lady approached me with, "Nancy, for a pastor's wife you wear your skirts too short." My response? I went home and shortened all my skirts. The young people cheered! And I learned I could be myself and still have the support of the people. That woman and I did communicate. I could talk to her and let her know just what I felt about something, and she didn't hesitate to tell me how she felt.

I was Nancy Karo; but when Lin died, I found myself becoming *Mrs. Lindon Karo,* trying to keep him alive, I guess. My identity became that of Lin's wife. When I spoke, it was as if I were keeping Lin and his memory alive.

Many nights my sleep was filled with dreams of Lin. Most widows and widowers have similar dreams. One dream became a turning point for me. In the dream Lin and I were running on a California beach. Lin was in front of me and I kept reaching out to him, trying to grab him. He turned to me and said, "Nancy, you've got to let me go!" I woke up crying. I thought, then, of that verse in Scripture in which Christ turned to Mary and said, "Do not cling to me, for I have not yet ascended to the Father." I had to let Lin go and I needed to become Nancy again.

Several things helped me. I had many interests, but how could they be used? I went to the North Central Career Development Center in New Brighton, Minnesota, where I completed ten hours of testing prior to a day and a half of intensive evaluation and counseling. I completed vocational interest tests, personality tests, and aptitude tests. The outcome was very helpful. The results of the vocational interest test showed that my highest interests were athletic and religious activities. In fact, my abilities aligned very closely with those of a *priest*! I knew I had to look over these interests and see where they could best be put to use.

The evaluation and counseling process was affirming for me. It was a day and a half spent talking about *me,* my interests, my abilities. It fixed in my mind who I was—a person of worth, with skills and abilities.

As I sat with my tests and remembered the counsel and evaluation, I was able to select clear goals. Because of my abilities and interests in religious activities and in athletics, I thought of our denomination's Trout Lake Camp, where I had already served as a counselor and teacher, and where I had been asked to be camp pastor for junior girls the next season. In my experience at Trout Lake Camp I had seen several areas of need. I went to the camp officials and told them of my ideas. They needed a coordinator of teaching and counseling, someone to hire counselors, coordinate curriculum materials, and prepare the people to use them. The director asked if I could begin the next day!

That year the boys and I spent the summer at the camp. It was a rich experience for all of us. It was so affirming to know that what I had prepared was useful. The program is still in operation, more finely tuned, but it is the program that I had envisioned and begun.

My next goal was to complete my college education. I had completed three years and up until now had had no desire to go on. Ten months later I received my B.A. It was another goal realized.

Lastly, I needed to publish the book I had begun. Now I earnestly struggled to complete the manuscript, have my friend Alvera edit it, and have it published.

The first publisher I sent it to returned it, saying that this was the third such manuscript recently received and they could not use it at the time. I was dejected. All that work for nothing?

Two friends helped. One told me he had received *ten* rejections for one manuscript! I don't know how encouraging that was, but I sure laughed and my mood changed abruptly! Another said, "Just think. How many people can say they even have been able to have a manuscript rejected!"

My book was finally accepted and I received the first copies in June of 1976.

Goals. At times they kept me going when other circumstances were crowding in on me. I knew it was important to work on something useful, creative. Set goals.

Through all this, I began to see that Nancy Karo had gifts and abilities that could be used. I had been a secretary for years and knew I could fall back on that, but I preferred other work.

Philippians 4:11 says, "I have learned to find resources in myself whatever my circumstances." I didn't realize how true that was. I had an added resource, an advantage because I am a Christian. Ephesians 1:19 says, ". . . how vast the resources of his power open to us who trust in him." I Timothy 6:6, 7: ". . . religion does yield high dividends, but only to the man whose resources are within him." My resources and God's resources.

I used one little exercise that helped. First I listed all my interests and abilities, who I thought I was. I made the list as long as possible; this list might be called "a brag sheet." That is hard for most of us Christians. We have an idea of false humility; we put ourselves down and never dare tell others anything good about ourselves, and don't even dare tell ourselves.

I bragged to me. The list was longer than I expected. I had talent. I was somebody.

I made another list of my major weaknesses. I limited it to three items. Usually we are good at drawing up a long list of these. I deliberately limited mine to three. I consolidated, crossed out, and came up with three major weaknesses. As I studied them, I saw that they were related. One was that I am a people pleaser. Another, that it is hard for me to say no. Right now I can't recall the third. With that list I took another piece of paper and listed goals to help me overcome those weaknesses. I added a bit on how to develop my strengths and accomplish some dreams. I can still look back on that exercise as one of the most beneficial things I did in discovering who I was, my identity. I wrote out some long-term goals and some short-term goals. This exercise has helped other persons who are alone after years of togetherness to find themselves as individuals.

We have the resources within ourselves whatever our circumstances.

9

Children Coping with Death and Divorce

A cceptance of the loss of a parent is a long time in coming. It may come sooner in a death than in divorce because of the finality of death.

When my boys lost their father through death, it was an experience they faced alone. None of their peers had lost a parent by death.

The morning after Lin died, I had to tell Steve and Rob that he was dead. They sat on the bed with me for a time. Steve's immediate need was to tell a friend, even if his friend wouldn't understand. He left early for school that day. He and Dave were going to walk. Soon, however, he came back home. "I told Dave Dad died." Now he had someone with him to face his schoolmates. They took the bus together, and Dave, unknowingly, gave Steve the emotional support he needed.

Rob needed to tell his teacher. He was upset because when he arrived at school she already knew. (I had called to explain in case any problems came up and the boys needed to come home.) Rob had cried some that morning, or at least he appeared to cry. I don't think he could tell me to this day whether or not they were real tears. He was only seven. A seven-year-old may think that is what should be done even if he doesn't *feel* like crying.

That day in school the class was asked to make cards for a classmate in the hospital. Rob told the teacher he would rather make one for his dad. It said, "To Dad From Rob." On it was a picture of a boy standing in a puddle of tears, saying, "I DIDN'T WANT YOU TO DIE." I now understand that children often show grief in actions rather than in words. Later, at the funeral home, Rob placed the card in his dad's pocket.

Scott was only three. Confusion would best describe his reactions. He questioned a lot! He came in later that morning after I had told Steve and Rob about Lin's death. He said, "We have to bury Daddy, don't we, because he died? We can't visit him at the hospital anymore because he's with Jesus. If we visit him, we'll have to visit him with Jesus."

When Steve and I went shopping the following day, Steve told me, "Dad said we shouldn't look back." I think that helped Steve to go forward. Then, after a time he added, "You know, Job suffered. He really suffered a lot, and he still believed in God."

Such comments and actions no doubt helped the boys, but they were hard on their mother!

A three-year old just blurts out what is on his mind. Some of the comments were rather funny.

> May 3, 1973. At nap-time Scotty asked to see "Daddy in the basket again." Close to what he meant, I guess. I again explained that Daddy's casket and body were buried. "Daddy is with Jesus and I know it is hard for you to figure that out." "Ya. What you said. But when I'm bigger I will!" Then he went on to tell how they buried the fish. Poor little guy, and his questions are quite frequent and troublesome for a three-year-old.

Perhaps the reality was that it was far more troublesome for me than it was for him.

Yet several days later he came into the house and asked, "When is Daddy coming back from heaven?" He had often experienced his dad returning from the hospital. No matter how much we tried to explain the permanency of death, he still wasn't able to grasp it.

October 26, 1973. Scotty's questions:

> "What if everyone dies, what will we do with the houses?"
> "What will we do with the baskets (caskets)?"
> "Where is all of Daddy?" (I then explained that Daddy's body died but the part that makes him live and walk and talk is with Jesus.) "What does he *do* with the other part that made him talk?"
> My explanation: "Jesus is keeping him alive with Him in heaven."
> "I wanted our daddy to live with us!"

"Is Jesus sitting here with us?"

I answered, "Jesus is everywhere."

"No. Jesus can't be here. Do you know why? Because He's keeping Daddy alive."

If Scott was most open, Rob was the most silent. He was there, listening to all that was going on, but he wasn't one to comment or ask questions. Maybe his pain and grief stayed inside a bit too long.

April, 1976. The boys and some friends and I were playing Pit. Rob lost. Steve's friend had just asked about Lin and the book (*Adventure in Dying* was about to be on the market) and what was in it about the kids. . . . and we talked about that. Soon Rob went to bed so I went in, thinking he felt badly about losing. He just sobbed and said, "You reminded me about Dad." So we both sat there crying. Now I feel teary . . . but for Rob mostly. So much has happened. It must really have hit him. It's hard to see your kids hurting.

May 1, 1976. Rob must be having a bad time. Tonight he asked, "Why did Dad have to die? There's no one to wrestle with." I mentioned Grandpa. He agreed that was fun, "but not as fun as with Dad." Grandpas are grandpas, not dads!

In 1977 we were in California visiting Lin's home church. I was speaking. It was a situation in which I felt I really should retell the events leading to Lin's death because of the church members' concern for us and because they had known him so well. We had begun our married life together as members there. After the service Lin's folks and the boys and I were going to buy sandwiches at a fast-food place. When I volunteered to drive to get the food, Rob said he would like to go along. In the car he opened up. "I cried when you were speaking, Mom. I thought about Dad. I think it's the first time I've really cried." *Four* years later. But thoughts and feelings were still there. He relived his dad's death. I think it was good for him.

It was some time before Steve cried, too. Weeks, though, rather than years. One evening he was missing his dad so much. I asked if he had cried. He said he hadn't. So I encouraged him to do so, mentioning that God gave us tears and that shedding them helps release the pain that is inside. "Sometimes when you need to cry and other people are around, just go up to your room where you can be alone. Maybe that might help."

The next morning he reported, "Last night I cried, Mom. I thought of 'Jesus Christ, Super Star' and the song, 'I Don't Know How to Love Him.' I don't know how to love Him. I prayed for Dad to be healed and he wasn't. It doesn't make sense."

"The main thing right now, Steve, is that you were able to cry—to get rid of some of that hurt inside. Maybe someday understanding will come. Maybe it won't. But it does help to cry when you need to."

Several months later, he had another experience. "Look what I just read," he said angrily. "'When he calls on me I will answer; I will be with him in trouble, and rescue him and honor him. I will satisfy him with a full life and give him my salvation' (Psalm 91:15, 16, *The Living Bible*). I prayed. He promised to answer. He didn't!"

"Well, look what *I* just read!" I added. "'He asked of thee life, and thou didst give it him, length of days for ever and ever.' (Psalm 21:4) Boy, it just doesn't make sense. I know Dad is healed completely because he's with Jesus. But that isn't what we meant when we prayed."

It was sufficient for Steve that I had struggled with Scripture too. I didn't have the answer, but someone else was where he was that day and it was okay.

A year after Lin's death, when Scott was four, he became almost possessed with thoughts of his dad.

> June 19, 1974. Scotty had done it again. On the way to Grantsburg he said, "If I cut my heart open (in response to the song, 'Open Up Your Heart and Let the Sun Shine in'), I'll die, won't I? . . . I think I'll cut my heart open because then I'll see Daddy and I'll kiss him."
>
> Later: "It's very sad." I asked what. "That our daddy died."
>
> Tonight praying: "Thank you, Jesus, for daddy, and make us die." He turned to me and continued, "I hope we die, don't you?"

My concern about Scott was great and I shared this with a friend. She suggested, "Maybe you should encourage him to pray for a new daddy and get his mind elsewhere." Now, I don't know how wise that was, but something had to change. The next time Scott said such a thing, I said, "Scott, maybe we should pray for a new daddy." He yelled, "Oh, boy! What should we call him?"

That ended the problem! Soon after this incident, I was going to a wedding. When Scott found out, he said, "Oh, good. If he's a daddy, can we keep him?"

Grief was different for each. Steve could verbalize his feelings somewhat. Scott asked questions. Rob was silent, maybe showing his grief in actions. Many children become overly restless, irritable, sometimes culminating in juvenile delinquency. Grief is rarely finished in children.

As much as I tried to be open with the boys during their dad's illness and after his death, there is still, seven years later, some grief work to be done. No doubt it couldn't be worked through because of their inability to communicate feelings, and my inability to be a mind reader and thus failing to offer support when it was needed.

But children are resilient. How they bounce back can depend on the love they sense and the support surrounding them.

An incident at school helped Rob. A new boy came to the school, shy, cautiously telling that his dad died. Rob nonchalantly said, "We're even. My dad died, too." Rob was able to express his feelings and help a new student gain composure in a new and unsure setting.

It helps to be able to help!

*   *   *

One in three marriages end in divorce (in California, it is one in two). The number of children involved in divorce has tripled in the last twenty years. Statistics are not getting better. Each year one million children are faced with a family unit dissolving. According to the February 11, 1980, issue of *Newsweek*, there are twelve million children under the age of eighteen whose parents are divorced. "Forty-five per cent of all children born in any given year will live with only one of their parents at some time before they are 18."[1]

Children of divorce face similar problems to those losing a parent by death, but there are unique problems: feelings of blame for the split; custody complexities; and a universal desire (no age barrier here) for the parents to reunite.

The authors of *Living in Step* have many practical insights into step-family relationships. Donny's experience is an example of a divorce reaction:

Donny would run along between both parents, one, two, three

swwwiiiiinnnnggg, Donny would swoop through the air. "Again! Again!" he'd shout. One, two, threee. . . .

It was all warm and happy. Mommy laughed a lot. Daddy would come home early and play bear on the rug, grumbling bear noises and rubbing him with his prickly whiskers. Daddy could do everything and would show him how.

There came the time, then, when Mommy stopped laughing and Daddy stopped coming home early. Bear! Bear! he'd shout, but Daddy and Mommy weren't hearing him. . . .

Then, one afternoon, he heard them fighting in the next room. Low voices getting louder and softer, all tough and edgy like sandpaper. He couldn't move; he stood there listening, holding his breath. Clear as a cannon, he heard Daddy: "How can you ask me to give up that wonderful boy?

The world stopped, and somewhere in the void he heard the word "Divorce! divorce! divorce!" crashing like so many waves of disaster. He'd never heard it before; he didn't know what it meant, but he knew it was horrible.

He was staring at his toy chest with the circus animals, red and yellow, marching bravely around it. Time stopped. The next thing he knew, Mommy and Daddy, together, were holding him, and he heard himself shrieking a high-pitched, tearing scream.[2]

An eight-year-old girl said in the *Newsweek* article "I remember it was near my birthday when I was going to be six that Dad said at lunch he was leaving. I tried to say, 'No, Dad, don't do it, but I couldn't get my voice out. I was too much shocked. All the fun things we had done flashed right out of my head and all the bad things came in. . . . The bad thoughts just stuck there. My life sort of changed at that moment. Like I used to be always happy and suddenly I was sad."

A nine-year-old girl said, "In a way, I thought I'd made it happen. I thought maybe I'd acted mean to my mother and my sister and I was being punished by God. So I tried to be really good by not waking Mom before schooltime and getting my own breakfast and maybe God would change His mind. But it's been three years now, and I'm used to it all. Sometimes, when I make a wish with an eyelash, though, I still wish for Dad to come home."[3]

In the past, the mother and the children usually lived together. Dad left. Not so now. The issue of custody is complex. The children can benefit from both parents giving them support. Yet, in order to gain joint custody, fathers in many areas still need to file for sole custody. Children can get caught in the middle even if both parents are amicable; their "placement" often rests solely on the decision of the judge.

In divorce, children tend to play one parent against the other. In cases where the divorce ends in a "battle," a parent can also use the children against the other parent, placing the children in the middle, at a time when they are struggling with fierce emotions new to them.

"Research has shown that the brunt of the shock can be lessened," say the authors in *Newsweek*, "for example, if the children are told about the divorce in a realistic way, if they are reassured about keeping in contact with both parents and if their daily routines are disturbed as little as possible."[4]

The authors of the article mention that a child's response to divorce varies according to age.

Toddlers between the ages of two and four . . . often regress in their development to a more dependent level. . . . In this age group, when sexual interest runs high, the removal of the parent of the opposite sex is thought by some psychiatrists and psychologists to be particularly detrimental to the child's sexual development. Children of this age-level seem convinced [they have] caused the divorce.

Children between the ages of six and eight also take on the responsibility for the split-up, but they have the additional fears of abandonment and often of starvation. "They are old enough to realize what is going on, but they don't have adequate skills to deal with it," explains John Tedesco, chief psychologist at the Des Moines Child Guidance Center in Iowa. Many experts agree that this is the most critical age for children of divorce—and it is the one with the largest number of children affected.

Between the ages of eight to twelve, the children's most distinguishing emotion is anger directed at whatever parent is thought to be the initiator of the divorce . . . The anger can erupt in classrooms and alienate friends just when they are most needed.

The teenagers, unlike younger children, feel little sense of blame . . . but they are saddled with what Tedesco calls the "loyalty dilemma." "Mom doesn't want me to like Dad, and vice versa."[5]

The common consensus in books and articles on divorce is that the children, no matter what their age, have an obsessive desire to reunite their parents.

One woman I know went to a band concert where her son was playing. At the coffee time her son came up with his father asking if the father could stay with them for the night.

"A nine-year-old New York girl spent all winter without a jacket on, trying to get sick enough so her parents would have to care for her—together. 'All I did was get a lot of colds,' she says ruefully."[6]

Children of divorce and children of the widowed face another problem that adults do not often consider—dating parents!

It is difficult enough for the parents to begin dating. The feelings of the children can be embarrassment, anger, jealousy, depression, or all combined. They may feel that the absent parent is being replaced. There can be the feeling of disloyalty to one parent if attention is shown to the "date."

Parents must take time to answer the questions children may raise and must reassure them of their continued love for and support of them.

Feelings and questions about themselves and the divorce bombard the children. Lovingly to take time with the children and explain some reasons for the divorce, to let them know they are loved by both parents and are not to be blamed, will bring reassurance. They should also be told, tactfully, that this is a permanent divorce, so they can be helped to face the finality of the separation.

Children can adjust. They can accept a new relationship and they can enjoy some of these relationships if they are included or feel included. Children are resilient.

Single— Dating—Sex

W e may have the resources within, but there are times when we wonder just where those resources might be.

Single again. Different from being alone. I now had a new identity. I was single in the couple's world of which I had been a part for so long. Questions bombarded me. What do I do with this loneliness that invades me at unexpected times? Does this loneliness affect dating? What about my sexual needs?

Loneliness crowds in during a busy day even though people are all around. It is there at night, when you pray with the children, tucking them into bed—alone, when you forget and set that extra place at the table, when you finally accomplish skiing on one ski and run to tell him and he isn't there! It was there when Steve made several touchdowns, winning the game for his team and the time Rob was pitching and single-handedly made a triple play, then proceeded to hit a grand-slam home run.

Loneliness is basic to grief. Grief comes from any loss whether it be by death or divorce. The church could have the answer to loneliness and I guess that is where we *want* the answer to be. It seldom is.

For the lonely, a sense of community is needed. Community involves shared concerns, shared problems, shared happiness. Our fear of rejection or judgment by such a community may cause us to withdraw just when we need that support most.

Bill Hulme of Luther Seminary in St. Paul said at a workshop, "The thought of being hurt again frightens you . . . prompts you to withdraw into a self-protecting shell . . . we choose loneliness because it seems less threatening." He said, "Lonely people sometimes try to shape themselves into pleasing personalities that others will like."

We become vulnerable. The formerly-married can be the most vulnerable because of their loneliness. We can be easily hurt. I know; I was hurt badly in one relationship.

What, then, is the way out of loneliness? We have heard that "solitude" is important. Loneliness vs. solitude. We have to face loneliness and not run from it, just as we must face pain and not try to mask it. As we struggle through our loneliness, listening to our inner struggles, we come from loneliness into solitude. I had my room to go to. I was getting to know me, struggling through grief and finally learning to enjoy being alone. Solitude. Blessed solitude.

Recently a man saw two cocoons, each with a butterfly struggling to free itself. He opened the cocoon of one. The butterfly flew away, but its color was less brilliant than the other. The man discovered that the beauty of the butterfly came in the struggle to get out of the cocoon.

Coming out of loneliness involves risk. We feel safer keeping to ourselves, even though we are lonely. Meeting someone new involves risk, as sharing more of ourselves involves risk.

John Brantner of the University of Minnesota said, "We can initiate casual encounters. We can learn to talk with strangers and can decide each time we go out whether today we will be an open, public person, or a closed, private person. Being open increases our alertness."

While traveling a few years ago I recall praying, "God, don't let anyone sit by me. I need to be alone." But on that plane trip God put on one side of me a frightened young boy who had never flown before. On the other side sat an elderly woman who had flown, but hated flying and was scared to death. She was sitting directly behind an open area with an exit door, increasing her fear. My needs became less important. I could have said nothing when my seatmates expressed their fears, but I chose to be an open person that day and it benefited us all.

Being single again, I needed close friends, at least one close friend. It is nice to have more than one, but we all need at least one person with whom we can share. I had friends who accepted me for who I was. I felt accepted by those who were not as close to me, but I soon learned that I was more acceptable because I had lost my husband through death and not divorce. In many Christian circles those who are single because of divorce are not so acceptable.

There are churches in which a divorced person cannot be a

member of a church board or teach Sunday school, or have a "public" ministry. It is good that this situation is changing and it must. These people are hurting as much as those who have lost a spouse through death. Instead of love and support, some churches give only condemnation and isolation.

"What effect did your divorce and remarriage have on your faith, on your religious experience?" Richard Krebs asked of Edie.

"Edie's eyes clouded over and she was quiet for a moment before she answered, 'It was awful. The church was the hardest place to be after my husband left. Sitting in the pew alone. Feeling guilty about being a divorced woman. If it hadn't been that I wanted my children to have a religious education, I think I might have left the church.'"[1]

I have yet to meet any couples who were happy about their divorce and the failure of their marriage. They are in pain. Divorce usually comes as a last resort, when everything else has failed. Often couples have tried counseling and trial separations, and togetherness. When all these fail, they move toward divorce. Divorce is second in stress only to death. The entire family suffers.

In many churches people just don't know what to say to a person who has been recently divorced. I know it is hard enough to know what to say to someone whose spouse has just died. Many divorced people are alone in churches, needing comfort and needing a friend.

A person I know telephoned a friend who was getting divorced and said, "I don't understand the why of your divorce, but I want you to know that I'm with you and that I care for you." That helped her friend on a day when many decisions had to be made, and none of them easy.

Divorced persons face alienation from the very people who could and should be of most help—the church family, the family of God, the community of believers.

They sense judgment from others: "They could have tried harder!" "It all started when *she* started working." In reality that may be what actually helped them stay together as long as they did.

Divorced persons face rejection. Perhaps a spouse left for someone else. Divorced persons may face an "ex" over and over again—sometimes with a lover, sometimes with a new spouse. Many divorced persons never wanted a divorce but were forced into it. Having friends to encourage one and to give support helps all newly single persons.

As a newly single person, dating is inevitable for most. Dating again. For me, at age 35, that had to be the most awkward situation I encountered. My first date was a very "safe" date. I had known him for years. He had been almost a part of the family. When he first asked me out, I didn't even consider it a date, I guess. We had good times together, and it stayed at the friendship level. Dating this old friend was a good way to break into a difficult situation because dating was so *new* again. I am glad for that good initial situation because there certainly were a lot of awkward ones that followed.

Have you ever tried to *avoid* someone? It isn't easy. No matter what you do, it seems the person you are trying to avoid is always there or always calling.

One man kept calling. Every time he called, he would say, "Hi, Nancy. This is 'Tom'" *Every* time I would say, "Tom? Tom who?" I hoped he would realize I wasn't interested when I couldn't even remember a last time or recognize a voice. Finally, I had to be more direct and say, "Tom, I don't think you should call any more because it seems that you are interested and I'm not."

Then there was Mr. Fixit. He would find fixable items around the house just to get in to talk, and talk, and talk.

Men who are single after losing a spouse have similar problems. After Darlene died, Emmett received a letter from one woman offering seven weekends that were available.

I had several conversations—good ones, by the way—with a recent widower who had five girls between the ages of 3 and 14. However, the prospect of being mother to eight children cooled that relationship.

One man called and called and invited me to every kind of function. I politely refused every invitation. Eventually I had to add my statement, "I don't think you should call because it seems that you are interested. . . ." Shortly after that I went to a retreat and the same man was there. I tried hiding. He found me as I sat in a corner, slinking down in my chair. He came sauntering over, put his hand on my shoulder, and said, "Hiya, Sunshine!"

On August 18, 1974 I recorded:

I thought before that dating might be appealing and now I wonder! Are any good situations around? Must remember what Betty [a friend] said, "Remember, there will be several disappointments, but don't give up. Keep going. You need these things."

On those first dates I felt worse than a teenager again. A teenager has peers to ask what to do, with whom to discuss problems, and ask advice. Silly questions confronted me: Where do you sit in the car? Next to the door, midway between door and date, closer to your date? Should I let him open my door in this new "women's lib" society? Is this the old-fashioned "men should pay" situation or is it the new "dutch-treat" era? Perhaps I should invite him in after the date, but I've heard sooo much about such situations.

Phil Donahue says, "There is no way in the world for a father of five children to describe the feeling of being introduced at age 39 as 'my boyfriend.' But that is how I was being identified by women who, for lack of a better word (and how I wish there were a better word), are called 'dates.'

"It had been 17 years since I had had a 'date,' and the only thing that hadn't changed was my wing-tipped shoes. It was like being back in college with gray hair. It was a *deja vu* nightmare in which all the old lines ('What's your major?') no longer worked. People who knew me would extend an arm for a 'How-ya-been?' handshake while staring at the woman next to me. The women next to me always seemed to be 24 years old, and I always seemed to be not so much shy as terrified."[2]

I enjoyed dating but wanted only companionship—no relationship developing. Unfortunately, most of the men wanted something more permanent.

You are warned that every man you date wants to go to bed with you. I did not find it so. I found that *I* had something to say in the matter and could control the situations. One fellow I had dated once suggested going into the bedroom, then suggested going camping, then proposed going on a mini-vacation. I refused every time. Finally he said, "You sure are old-fashioned! I don't agree with you, but I do respect your convictions."

This is not an easy area for a formerly-married person. Formerly married persons have been sexually active. Lin and I had a good thing going sexually. For the first year after his death, it was not a problem for me. But we are sexual beings. Thoughts and desires do return. For some the problem develops quickly after the loss.

I remember dreams I had frequently. We would be making

love. The frustration of waking up and not being fulfilled was overwhelming. I finally pleaded with God, "Please don't let me dream anymore. I can't take it!" God answered my prayer.

Researchers have compiled statistics on the difference between men and women in the frequency of sexual thoughts. I'm not sure of the exact figures but it was something like: Most men have a sexual thought about every 20 minutes and most women about every 20 hours. One pastor said he had great guilt feelings when he had these thoughts at the most inopportune moments, such as while singing the doxology or just before the sermon.

What are we to do? There aren't too many classes on "The Sexual Dilemma of the Single"!

We are sexual beings with sexual thoughts and desires. Scripture can be of help to some and it can also be a puzzle. What does it mean in Galatians 5;20, 21 where it says that fornication, impurity, and indecency are a part of the lower nature and "that those who behave in such ways will never inherit the kingdom of God." I Thessalonians 4:3 says, "You must abstain from fornication." I Corinthians 6:18 says to "flee or shun fornication." The dictionary defines fornication as "sexual intercourse outside of marriage."

Christianity Today published an article on "Sex and Singleness the Second Time Around," by Harold Ivan Smith. Researchers asked 203 formerly marrieds (146 women and 57 men) this question: "How many times have you had sexual relations in the last year?"

According to the results, "only 9 percent of the men and 27 percent of the women were celibate, although many noted the intimacy had been with only one partner and/or in a 'serious' relationship.

"It is worth noting that 67 percent of the men and 58 percent of the women reported a conflict between their faith and sexual experiences:

"'Sometimes I feel so despondent after having been out— having a good time in companionship and sexually—that I feel like I want to die rather than live this torn-apart feeling.'

"'. . . I felt the need to prove my sexuality to myself and to other men . . . but that inner conflict between my sexual needs and moral and spiritual needs still tears away at me. One part of me says that it is right and beautiful. The other part tells me that as a Christian, I should not be doing it.'"

Smith says, "Clearly, tension exists among those seeking to integrate two positions traditionally held to be opposing."[3]

Each person must decide how to handle his or her sexual desires. Some find that making a list of pros and cons helps them make this difficult decision: Having sexual intimacy and living with the guilt; or practicing sexual abstinence and living with the frustation.

The conflict remains. It still is up to the individual to struggle with his or her sexuality, decide what his or her convictions are, and stand by those.

Talking with someone? Yes, it does help to talk with one who has been there and really understands, someone who doesn't come up with pat answers but will listen as you struggle through this dilemma.

People have said, "Exercise!" True, exercise does release some tension but not permanently. Exercise is good, but it isn't the full answer when you begin caring for another person again.

I have a dear friend in her sixties. She shared her struggles with me regarding her own sexual needs. She was "seriously" dating a man and said that they would be together ten minutes and she'd be ready to run off to the bedroom. Age is not a consideration regarding our sexual needs. In her words, "I am very physical." And I guess I am, too.

Very few formerly married persons would be critical of others regarding their sexual experiences. Maybe there is nothing the church can do, but it can be aware and understand the unique situation of those who find themselves single the second time around. We need people who are available and not judgmental.

Discovering more about who we are and knowing what we believe does help. My exercise on listing my interests and abilities—good things about me—and my negative aspects, and then setting goals to aid in overcoming those negatives helped. I began to see who I was. I began to like me, to establish what I wanted in life.

Being with others helped. It was fun to get together with groups for social activities. I needed the fellowship. But we live in a couples' society. Perhaps no other institution is so couples oriented as the Christian church. We have the young married couples' class, the couples' bowling parties and the couples' roller-skating parties, not to mention the sweetheart banquets and Christmas parties for couples only.

I wasn't a couple. I needed couples. Those who are married

tend to invite other couples for dinner or coffee forgetting that singles need to be included. Singles often seem to be the forgotten people.

Churches also have many "single" married people in the congregations; only the wife or the husband comes to church. These people should also be remembered.

I talked to a divorced woman from a fine evangelical church. She was depressed and very lonely. The church was having a "couples' bowling party." That automatically left out my friend. She was by nature quite withdrawn, but that time she got up enough courage to ask the coordinator of the class party if she could go along. He answered, "I'm sorry, but this is for couples only." What a blow for her and what a missed opportunity for the church. The coordinator was not being malicious, just thoughtless.

I had some good friends who always remembered me. Whenever Ann and Marv Anderson had get-togethers I was invited. We went out to eat together, we played racquetball together. They included me and I them. They are among my closest friends.

One couple I knew well would invite me out to eat with them. But they were in school and I knew their budget was limited. We made a deal. If they would include me, I would pay my own way. It could have been awkward but they made it easy.

The single-again have needs. They must face many things alone. They experience loneliness at times. They find themselves in a new world of dating, of being sexual beings. The couples' world where there was comfort before is now strange.

The problems are many, the answers are few. But God and His people are (or should be) available.

Single Parent

I was alone, a single parent. Single parenting is common in today's society, but that does not make it any easier.

I had three young boys. Sometimes it frightened me to think of the responsibility I had in raising those boys, God's gift and fine gifts, to maturity. I often wondered, "Just what is maturity and is it ever reached?"

Day after day, night after night, there were questions I couldn't answer. Some I couldn't even understand.

On Memorial Day, 1973, I recorded:

I don't want to be the decision-maker, the sole "rearer" of three boys, the only one to whom they bring problems—no one to blame but me. I've just done a lot of thinking. My thoughts come out fuzzy on paper.

One episode I wrote down on August 25, 1973.

At dinner Scotty asked, "Why can't Daddy come back from heaven?" I tried to explain. Then he said, "Do you know why I want him to come back? So he can hold me." All I could do was choke out, tears running, "That makes me sad."

On September 29 I prayed and wrote,

"I do have a real concern for my boys and need much, much help. They're impressionable and I want the impression good. Thank you for caring for us. Let me remember that always."

God cares for us. I had to remember that during difficult times.

A line from a story in *McCall's* caught my eye. "The responsibility for them was too much on her shoulders; it ate into her love for them."[1] A single parent has no relief from the responsibilities. I felt I understood what the writer was talking about.

Phil Donahue wrote on "Coping Alone,"

> I thought about all the women in America who were raising children alone, without benefit of live-in help and without benefit of my income, and I realized one more feature of the culture's double standard. Women in my circumstances are expected to raise children *and* money without applause. When men do it, they are showered with attention and admiration, and if they're lousy at it, they take on the "little boy lost" aura, which makes them even more attractive.
>
> When I think of the countless women in this country who get up in the morning, make breakfast, see that the children are dressed properly, send them off to school, dress, go to work, come home, make dinner, speak to the emotional needs of the children, do the wash, and get up again in the morning only to do it all over again, I don't know how they do it."[2]

I thought of my friend with the five girls all so young, without live-in help, having to tell them the facts of life, ironing pretty dresses, and my heart went out to him. The "little boy lost aura"? Maybe so.

September 24, 1974. A really fine day. Came home, prayed with Steve and Scott. Scotty prayed, "And I hope we get a new dad soon." Steve mumbled, "I don't want a new dad."

October 11, 1974. Today Scotty got a birthday card in the mail from Lin's mother and as I read it to him he was grinning from ear to ear. As I finished, he blurted out, "I bet my daddy sent that!" And I burst into tears, barely able to choke out that it was from Grandma.

Steve was forever breaking bones. I went to his hockey game one Sunday and saw a head-on collision. Steve stood up. His nose was on the other side of his face, or so it seemed. I was very frightened.

I called our orthopedic surgeon (I felt that he was "ours" by now). He calmed me and told me to take Steve to the hospital for X rays. Maybe nothing further would have to be done.

Yes, his nose was fractured and, no, the surgeon did not have to do anything to it. It looked bad, but when the swelling went down, it was back to normal!

Once while I was at a parent-teacher conference, I was given a message that one of my children had fallen off the rafters in the garage and it appeared that his wrist was broken. I didn't even ask which child. It would have to be Steve. Everything that happened like that had been Steve so far.

I excused myself from the conference and went home. It was Steve and his wrist was broken.

This year when Rob broke his wrist for the second time, and the doctor in attendance at the hockey game put on a splint, he turned to me and asked if I would be okay driving Rob to the hospital alone. I answered him, "I'm fine. I have three boys."

It is hard to have no one to share responsibility or hurts. It is also hard not to be able to share joys.

An interesting thing happened at a play-off baseball game. Rob was pitching and kept making fine plays. A woman who knew me turned to me and said, "Someone up there is watching." I naturally thought she meant God. Then she said, "Do you see him? Lin?"

October 24, 1973. Tonight Rob received Christ. That should be a perker-upper! When I came in he jumped up and said he wanted to become a Christian. We talked for some time and then prayed together—my mom and dad kneeling with us in the living room.

It was good to be able to share such joys with my parents, but it wasn't quite the same as sharing them with Lin.

Many times I felt paranoid, wondering what people thought of me as a mother. I was especially conscious of what the church family thought of me as a mother. If I didn't feel like getting the boys ready for church on Sunday nights and left them home, someone was sure to ask why the boys weren't in church. I had to ask myself, "Whom am I pleasing? Them or me?"

Actually, there were only one or two people who upset me in this way. Most were very encouraging. One of the nicest things I heard was when one of the men said to me, "You have *such* nice boys!" You don't know what it meant for me to have him tell me that. I could have hugged him. Maybe I did.

August 1, 1973. Tonight I was reading *Lord, Could You Make It a Little Better?* It had the neatest poem:

> When we fail or lose or give up,
> let us not condemn
> but comfort each other

and encourage each other
to begin again.

Set us free from what has been
and what might have been
to live for what may be.
Give us a hope, Lord,
and restore to me a future.[3]

That is great. I needed that!
Occasionally I experienced real feelings of jealousy.

October 22, 1973. I just read some in James—speaks of
faith and action, the danger of the tongue, watch out for
jealousy. That's easy to be lately—especially seeing men
with their boys.

It would especially hurt me when I saw tenderness between
a son and his father.

August 25, 1973. Oh, my, another night with swollen
eyes. It started at the hockey game. A teammate, Rich,
simply asked the coach if Steve could play center and the
coach shushed them. Then Rich's dad went down and chat-
ted with Rich, patting him on the back. Just that fatherly
gesture and the tears had to be blinked away.

Jealousy wasn't a constant thing, but now and again it did
come to me.

I had said once, "The boys need a dad so much and I feel
inadequate to be both mom and dad to them." I am not a mom
and dad. I am a mom and I wonder at that at times. Maybe
chauffer, nurse, psychologist, arbitrator, or counselor would be
better. I *did* things, and I know I gave them a lot of love. I felt
love so that was no problem.

As a child, I recall men doing things for women. But now I
was *doing* for everyone as far as the boys could see, but no one
was *doing* for mom. How could they see what husband-wife
relationships should be? I think they would have made poor
husbands—good fathers, poor husbands! Oh, they all had their
own responsibilities inside and outside of the house, but they
never *saw* anyone doing anything for mom. They had no model.

I had always thought that because the boys had no father,
they had no male image. What is really true is they have neither
a male nor a female image.

It wasn't until after Emmett and I were married that our boys began to see that things could be done for moms. Once when we were going out in the evening, I had to run to the store. I was going to hurry back so I could soak in the tub for awhile— one of my favorite things. I returned from the store and Steve was eagerly waiting for me. It was unusual because I knew he, too, was going out for something that evening. He and the other boys just kept following me around. I finally entered the bath- room and saw that Emmett had filled the tub to the brim with hot water, just the way I like it. The lights were out and candles were flickering on the tub and around the room. There was a dish of strawberries (with cream and sugar!) on the side of the tub. And a dish of M & Ms! It was a fantastic model for three boys. They saw a man doing something nice for a woman.

I think I had an advantage growing up when I did and in the church setting that I did. Almost every Sunday evening families would be invited into homes of other families in the church. We don't do that much now. It is mostly "adults only, please." And there isn't even much of that.

When I rebelled, I did not rebel against the church. I remember the people of the church liked me and I liked them. God was in those people. But I did rebel against my parents—for what, I couldn't really tell you. But the church was there even through my rebellion. I had a chance to see parenting modeled through other parents. My boys didn't have that opportunity so much. They did see role models in homes of their friends, however. I remember Steve coming home saying, "I'm sure glad I grew up in a good home." Some "non-Christian" act had taken place in the neighborhood. He'll never know how much that comment meant to me.

As a single parent, my least favorite program in the church I attended was called "Boys' Brigade." It is a sort of church- oriented, Christian boy scouts without the camping experiences. It was really a father-son organization. The worst time of the year was Pinewood Derby time when the boys and dads made goofy little cars. I mean, they had to *carve* the cars, paint and decorate them, put the correct weights someplace, and have a race. Guess who lost?

One man did help Steve for a similar race—rockets. Steve came in second. He was thrilled and I was so grateful to Bob Kendall who took time with my son to help him with a project in which I felt lost.

I was out no matter how you cut it. For mother-daughter teas and banquets, I had no daughter. Fortunately, I was one. At least in the girls' program there was a prayer-partner situation where women were matched with girls from the club. I could pray for a girl even if she weren't my daughter. There were prayer-partner teas and other functions, so women without daughters and girls without mothers were included. I wonder why the boys' leaders never thought of such a thing.

I have been trying to ascertain just what was done to aid my children in facing a fatherless home. A big thing for Steve was not having anyone to help him with his sports. He and Lin had spent a lot of time together playing ball. I wrote on March 14, 1974:

> Good grief. I've spent much of the day in tears and Steve just came in telling of his loneliness and a dream he had last night. He even said he thought, "Why didn't Billy Graham [awful thought here but I was glad he knew of the influence of Billy Graham] die instead of Dad? Dad was such a good preacher. And he always did everything with us. He showed me how to play baseball and football— everything. I just felt empty last night."
>
> "Holy Father, I need You and Your comfort—I need cotton tonight."

I wasn't good at pitching and was worse at football! One thing that helped Steve was that he took it upon himself to help Rob in these things. He wasn't too much of an expert at age eleven, but he was doing something for someone else. It helped.

I didn't try to be Lin, to be a father to the boys. I was their mother. However, I was active and I loved sports, so that helped.

I did have to make my sons aware of certain problems. Even though I didn't want to give the impression that a single-parent family is "different," there are precautions that need to be clear. I listed my telephone as N. Karo, not Nancy Karo. When the boys answered the telephone and were asked for their dad, they were taught to say, "He's not here, would you like to speak to my mother?" Or, "He's not here right now, my mother will be back in a few minutes, could I have her call you?"

Steve had received a couple of calls harrassing him. Maybe someone saw the obituary. Sad, but there are sick people in our society who will even harrass children when they are already in pain. If Steve had known how to answer the telephone, the callers might not have continued the conversation.

I knew that in order to help the boys, I had to help myself. As a single parent there was no one to relieve me from the constant responsibility. Some evenings I just had to get away from that responsibility by getting a babysitter and going to dinner or to a movie with friends.

One "single-again" woman had potluck dinners and would invite one or two families. As a result her children had regular contact with other families and those families included her and the children at other social gatherings. Had she not taken that step, she and her children might have been sitting home a lot more.

As a single-parent family, we began doing things together. Monday was our family night. I budgeted for this even when there was little money available. I felt that strongly about it.

We took up skiing. A little hilly area in the Minneapolis-St. Paul area offered skiing lessons for a nominal fee. Steve and I took the lessons. Rob tried skiing on his own on smaller hills and Scott went sliding. The following year,when Scott was five, Rob nine, and Steve twelve, we took to larger hills and we all skied. Frequently we would take several other kids along. We sometimes had eight kids and all the skis in my little Pinto wagon. But we had fun.

Sometimes we went out to eat on Mondays. There we were confined to a table and we had to talk with one another. That "talk time" was also valuable in solidifying us as a family.

We didn't dwell on "what might have been." Lin was gone. That could not be changed. "What might have beens" can be devastating. I knew we had to take our emotional capital of the past and reinvest in the future.

We all gained new skills, new interests, and established our new family bond and identity. We grew alone, grew independently, and collectively.

Edgar Jackson says of a child, ". . . he will be influenced by the expression of feeling of the adults around him . . . hysteria breeds hysteria.

"If a family talks with composure, explaining to children in a language they can understand that someone they loved is not going to be there anymore, the child accepts the quiet expression and responds in a similar fashion."[4]

A friend of mine told me how her dad had died at a very early age. When the hearse came for the body, my friend was locked in the chicken coop and told her dad was gone for a while. She was not allowed to attend the funeral. Only in recent years has she been able to face the death of her father.

Honesty—answering the questions the children ask, maybe not more than they ask, but answering what they ask—helps bridge the gap between their understanding and grief and helps them face the fact that the loss of their parents is permanent.

I never said, "This is God's will." Maybe it was. I couldn't figure that concept out. How could I expect my children to? God's will that their father die—what kind of God is that? My God had been there during all my struggles and difficult times. I wanted my children to feel that their God was there, too. Maybe Lin's death didn't make any sense, but God would walk with us through this.

Our boys were helped by the sports in which they were involved. We were with baseball, football, and hockey parents once in a while.

There was no father in our home. In some other homes there is no mother. We were a single-parent family. I was mother, and mother only. The boys had to accept the fact that they had no father. But we were still a family. We had those resources within ourselves upon which to draw. We were having good times. It was okay.

ᴸ5ᴼ⁴

Remarriage—
Stepparenting

After a year or so without Lin, I had learned to enjoy my singleness. Dating was fun. Independence was an interesting experience. I was used to being a single parent and was learning to cope with that responsibility.

As I became even more independent, I worked on growth. God had given me abilities and I wanted to develop and use those gifts.

I had struggled with some of the decisions that needed to be made by a single person, but I learned to enjoy making many of those decisions.

I was feeling very good about Nancy. I was whole. Life was good.

Then came Emmett Johnson.

When I was aware that a relationship with Emmett could be headed for something more serious, I was excited but also afraid. Joy, pain, fear, excitement all mixed into one.

I recall the first time Emmett called. He phoned late one evening. We had talked on the phone for nearly an hour when he said, "Do you serve widowers coffee?"

He came over and we talked a long time. He was lonely and he needed to talk. His pain over the loss of his wife, Darlene, was still severe. He knew I understood where he had been and where he was now. We talked and we both cried.

After he left, I cried. "He's going to die, too. It isn't fair. It isn't fair!" The previous November Emmett had had a recurrence of Hodgkin's disease that had first been diagnosed ten years before. For nine years he had been cancer-free. He was now undergoing chemotherapy. Just from the time we spent that evening, I recognized what kindred spirits we were. But I knew, too, that I could not go through another ordeal with cancer. Nor could the boys. Even if I felt I could handle it, I vowed I would not put the boys through another loss. I was *not* going to get involved. It was a logical conclusion, but my feelings would not go along.

We began seeing each other, but I was on the defensive. Any time I felt myself getting close, too involved, I would stiffen. "I can't hurt again. Not like I did before."

Emmett could sense that I was detaching myself. It was hard on him. Things would be going just fine and all of a sudden here comes old cold-fish Nancy again. I was scared.

I knew, too, that we had differences to consider as we went from casual dating to developing a relationship.

How had each of us related to our former spouses? How had we communicated? What were housekeeping "roles" and habits? How did we relate to children? What were our methods of discipline?

These are complex issues.

I didn't realize how many fears I had. We continued to date on a regular basis. Yet it wasn't until several months later that I put down my defenses and let myself love again. Nearly a year later, Emmett and I were married.

Remember those "big" adjustments when you were first married: like who takes out the garbage, how we define our "roles" when both are working full time.

Guess what. Adjustments are even greater the second time around.

Emmett and I both are strong personalities. By the time we began dating, I felt "whole." I had been growing, yet I wanted to continue to grow and not be dominated or squashed. How we had related to our former spouses could help or hinder that growth process.

In our first marriages both Emmett and I were in our twenties. We had learned with our spouses. We had grown together, learned to relate in particular ways; our communication with our spouses was learned and known. We were not at all set in our ways. Our first marriages had been a gradual getting-to-know-each-other process—mine lasting 12 years, Emmett's for 25 years.

Emmett and I came into this relationship and marriage with different values. Our ways of relating to our spouses had been different. Communication had been different.

Naturally, our similarities had attracted us to each other. We both love life. We love people and are comfortable in most situations. We enjoy excitement. We are both impulsive. One of us can suggest something and away we go. We both like the excitement of that kind of life.

There were adjustments that we did not consider. We were on an emotional high. Life was full and exciting, and the differences would take care of themselves. We thought, "After all, we are mature individuals who have gone through the adjustments of marriage. We can handle it."

We needed to learn that when problems come—and they will—in remarriage, even though they may seem insurmountable, they are "normal." We are not alone. Others, I'd venture to say *all* others, have the same problems (if they would only admit to it!).

After remarriage, it does take time for everyone to adapt. There are so many *major* adjustments. Many times I would say again, "I need more cotton, Lord." I had known the pain of singleness. I had learned how to handle singleness and enjoy it. New relationships take work and time for growth. There can be pain in that. Yet in the pain of growth, there is strength and healing.

Communication. I had read and reread John Powell's *Why Am I Afraid to Tell You Who I Am?* I liked and believed what he said— in theory. In fact I tried to practice it. But if I found myself on the defensive, all learning went down the drain and my feathers ruffled.

The June before Emmett and I were married, I wrote in my journal the following:

A rough time between Emmett and me because a person came over and a couple of misplaced comments were made. And then I guess we had a "learning" time, if that's what you want to call it. He was hurt and because of the way remarks were given, I became angry. Then it became a battle of wits and tears. We saw what was going on and did get it all talked out but I was beginning to wonder if we really could make it through disagreements. It ended fine—good, in fact. Growth came and we've agreed on a few things that will help us in the future. Principles of communication came back—too late, but soon enough to be able to evaluate what I was doing and to be able to see my emotions and reactions.

Some principles we decided on: Keep in the first person,

singular—"I" feel, rather than "You do or should or are.
. . ." Stick with feelings rather than bring judgment on the
other.

Those principles are good. Too bad that in the heat of emotion
we sometimes forget them. We have communication differences.
Most of us "remarrieds" do have real struggles in learning to
communicate together. We have done things one way and even
if we did not like that way, it was comfortable. Unlearning some
things. Relearning others. It's tough.

From the start Emmett and I tried not to avoid issues. We had
many discussions and sometimes they were heated.

About six months after we were married, we had our first
major confrontation, about the use of a credit card.

All learning went. We were each on our own trying to
"outwit" the other. The result: hurt.

However, we didn't *ignore* our feelings. We talked and talked,
but something still was not right. I wasn't angry anymore, but
I was still hurt. There we were, two people hurting and neither
really responding. It wasn't resolved that night.

The next day talk continued. Finally, Emmett asked, "How
are you?" I answered, "Hurt." Our talking then began on a
different level. His "How are you?" was a genuine question
wanting a genuine answer. He heard my "I hurt" and we were
able to communicate.

We found out there were things that had been hidden for
some time that neither of us was aware of until that in-depth
talk. When things are not discussed in early stages, they build
up.

Finances in remarriage. Together Emmett and I had homes,
furniture, dishes, supplies for two houses. We both had in-
comes; mine was very limited so there wasn't a huge problem
there!

We did have advice before we were married regarding money
matters. Ours were not complicated. Some are.

Children may be concerned about heirlooms or those special
things that belonged to the parent who died.

Before Emmett and I were married, he gave Keith things he
felt were important family mementos. Keith chose others that
were meaningful to him. Of the items Emmett kept, the family
heirlooms will eventually go to Keith. This was decided upon
prior to our marriage.

There may be two people marrying, both of whom have important positions. One is about to be transferred. What do they do then? Realistically talking about the situation and getting counsel from a trusted advisor can be of help.

Both parties may have homes. Hers may be roomier, his more convenient to his place of employment, hers recently decorated, his payments lower. Perhaps selling both homes and buying one that was chosen together and decorated together would alleviate the problem.

Emmett and I sat down with a lawyer prior to our marriage and again after we were married to set up our wills. We benefited from the advice of the one who counseled us concerning our finances. Good, practical advice is to settle as many financial matters as possible prior to remarriage. There are enough other adjustments (such as disposing of furniture and furnishings, emotional adjustments, and adjustments with blending families) that come on the scene that cannot be programmed!

It is important to accept the fact that there will be problems. Irritations that arise during dating become greater after marriage. It is good to come to terms with them, to accept them.

One good bit of advice is to write down all the qualities that you loved about each other while dating. Keep the list handy for those later times when you are ready to strangle your mate!

Darrell Sifford interviewed Ray E. Short who feels strongly that premarital sex is wrong and only leads to marital problems, but he says, "No couple should enter marriage without spending a weekend together camping—so the woman can see how the man reacts when he hooks a big fish but slips on a wet rock, cracks his tailbone and loses the fish. That can tell her more about him than a year of dating. The man," Short said, "can get more than a few clues when he sees how the woman reacts when rain blows into the tent and her hair and clothing get wet and she looks like a drowned rat."[1]

Prior to remarriage, settle finances, know your differences and accept them, date long enough to know how the other reacts in both favorable and unfavorable circumstances, and consider children: "yours" and "mine" and will there be an "ours"?

Children are important to parents. We value them and we value our relationships with them. This was a concern for me. Emmett had one quiet son, now grown. I had three active young children, who had each other to blame, to bicker with, sometimes to fight with. I was used to the noise, the busyness of a household that usually had six or so boys wandering in and out. Noise. Boys. Many of them! Constant activity. All new to Emmett.

Yet he tells of a Father's Day alone. He and his son, Keith, had moved into a townhouse days before. He was trying unsuccessfully to hang drapes. Keith had just left to visit his best friend. Even the dog was gone. Knowing Emmett was alone, I called and asked if he would like to spend Father's Day with us. I was having my brother's family (two children), my parents, and my sister's family (five children) for dinner. Ten kids! He cautiously accepted.

Somehow, in coming home from church, we forgot Rob, my twelve-year-old. Emmett went back to get him. Rob was standing at the church. Sometimes Rob had been quite rude to Emmett. I remember telling him once, "Rob, I don't ask that you like Emmett, but I do ask that you not be rude." Rob was the middle child. He was my protector! He seemed to see Emmett as someone invading his rights, invading his father's rights. He was very loyal to me and very loyal to his father.

When they came back, Emmett dropped Rob off and returned to his townhouse to change clothes. Rob said, "You are coming back, aren't you?" Emmett couldn't figure out the friendliness.

Rob began pacing back and forth, inside and outside, waiting for Emmett to return. When he arrived, Rob ran out and handed him a Father's Day card and a present. He had purchased these on his own. The card said, "To a Special Friend," and inside was written, "You're neat, Emmett." Emmett spent some time blinking!

It turned out to be one of his best Father's Days—noise and bedlam and caring. As Emmett said, "Consider the trade-off! I'd exchange it any day for the tick-tock of the clock on my wall."

Emmett was concerned about his own son, Keith. Even though Keith was twenty-two, Emmett wasn't sure how he would react to his dad's dating.

I think Keith's first reaction was that of relief. He and Brenda (now his wife) were "father-sitting" almost nightly. They would stay home and study or watch television to keep Emmett company. When we began dating, that brought relief.

Soon, however, I began to sense that something was amiss when I was with Keith and his dad. I couldn't understand why. I wondered if Keith's grief for his mother had been renewed or whether he wondered what place he now had in his dad's life. I didn't know and Keith and I didn't discuss it.

I was keenly aware that Keith's mother kept that significant place with him. After Emmett and I were married, I would be Keith's father's wife, not his mother. At his age, I wouldn't even be a stepmother to him.

As Keith and I were together more, I felt the relationship between us grow to be warm and caring. Getting to know him was fun. My boys also quickly learned to love Keith and I sensed a mutual caring there. Keith had a grand time teasing them— and me! Scott thought Keith was the strongest person around. "I'll bet he can lift 500 pounds," said Scott several months after Emmett and I began dating.

We soon saw that Emmett and I had different ways of relating to children. Discipline methods were far apart.

When Emmett fell in love with me, he did not necessarily fall in love with my children. Yet remarriage involves the whole family. We come in a package, with children, in-laws, value systems.

In every remarriage where children are involved, both partners must come to terms with the children.

It is important to discuss the way each feels a child should be disciplined and how to relate to children. It is helpful to know how each was raised as a child and what may have been done differently with each person's children. The more that is settled prior to marriage, the less severe any problems will be; but there will be problems.

Emmett became a stepparent. The boys became stepchildren.

In a remarriage the children may have already experienced the loss of one parent. They have learned to adjust to that loss. But now they are required to accept and (unspoken, but it is there) love the new parent. Since early childhood they have learned that they are to obey and honor their parents—and *love* them.

Brenda Maddox, in *The Half-Parent*, says, "Nearly one million children under the age of eighteen see a parent remarry, and well over half a million adults suddenly find themselves to be that curious figure, a stepparent." She states that "in the United States each year upwards of 400,000 children lose a parent through death. There even were, at the time of the 1970 census, 50,000 children under the age of ten who were living with a widowed father."[2] Those figures, coupled with the one million children each year being faced with a parent leaving because of divorce, make one stand in awe at what children and marrying parents face.

Children have fears. A fear that looms large for a child is "will my stepparent like me? Will he or she be my friend? Can I talk to him or her and be heard?"

"Old fears come alive, and new fears join forces with them. 'Who am I now? Where do I belong? Does my parent remarrying still love me? Will I lose my mother/father to this person he/she is remarrying? Can I like this new stepparent and still love my other parent (whether alive or dead, by the way)?' A whirl of uncertainties surrounds the child. The fears are there. Usually they are reinforced rather than calmed in the new marriage."[3]

How do we help the children?

The busyness the parent is caught in, the excitement, plans for marriage, may reduce attention to the children when the need is the greatest. I assumed, I am sure, that my relationship with my boys would remain the same. I learned that is not true. Their place in the family was being threatened. More attention, not less, was needed. A family time would be valuable where questions could be asked freely and discussions continue on an open level.

Because the children will be there, and one is marrying into the family—children, dog, and all—it would be wise to get to know those children well during the dating stage. Find mutual interests. There may be none. If the children are sports nuts (my boys) and the new spouse is not (like Emmett), the new spouse needs to be honest and open about that. Explain why. The new spouse can ask what their interests are and see if they might not be interested in one area where he or she shines. One of the "other" interests Emmett and the boys discovered was hunting. Emmett knew about hunting! The boys were interested and he could help them.

It helps if one gains insights into the family structure to see how the members "work" collectively and individually. One can see how the children relate in the family setting. Strengths and weaknesses will probably show. A talk over a Coke or a sundae might help. It is important to learn to relate to the children. Learn to like the children. Love breeds love.

Emmett took each of the boys someplace—alone—gaining a little understanding of the boys and they of him.

The authors of *Living in Step* say that in entering into the marriage, "the new stepparent may overdiscipline, overdo, or just plain overwhelm in an effort to build the instant relationship."⁴ It seems that a cautious, caring approach would be better.

Richard Krebs says, "It takes time for everyone to adapt to new roles after remarriage. Neither Edie nor Bill was rushing things. They were wisely giving the loving relationship with the children (and the dog) a chance to become solid before testing it with an authority relationship."⁵ Earning the rights of parenthood and the trust seem to be important.

For children of divorce, remarriage represents loss of hope; now Mom and Dad *can't* get together. Remarriage of one of their parents signifies an ultimate loss for them. Resentment could be strong and more cautious loving concern might be needed than anticipated.

The young children may have permanent or occasional (weekend) stepbrothers and stepsisters to contend with. Some may get along very well, but this is not common. One who was used to being the oldest may be the middle child now. One child may be neat, and gain a slob for a stepsibling and be expected to share the same room. Children in an original family often have problems in these areas. When Emmett and I were married, two of our boys had to begin sharing the same room. One was neat, one not neat. They might permanently dislike each other if they had to live that way all their growing-up years!

Then, there is the problem of teenagers of different sexes becoming *too* friendly!

What about children out of the home and on their own? In our situation, Keith planned to remain in the townhouse he and Emmett shared. Keith would be marrying soon after we were married.

Just as Emmett had to consider his relationship with my sons, I had to anticipate what relationship I would have with Keith. We became a blended family. Even though Keith would be married and live elsewhere, we were still a family. As questions come up, Keith still consults his dad. Keith and I have discussions. His wife, Brenda, and I have hilarious times. We are apart geographically, but we are a blended family with relationships that continue to develop. My last Mother's Day card from Keith was "To My Other Mother." I liked that!

Sometimes stepparenting seems hopeless. The one thing a stepparent does not have is good memories that can carry the natural parent through a crisis. Many times a stepparent lives from crisis to crisis without those memories to help. Stepparenting can usually work, but it takes time—lots of time.

Ginnie and her stepfather in *Living in Step* had a particularly stormy relationship but sought counseling. When asked what she would tell an about-to-be stepchild, she responded:

> I would say that it will be rough at first, but it's going to be the best experience that ever happened to you, that you are going to realize a lot of things about people. Looking at it now, this new marriage is really a good experience, despite the hassle we've had. You lose something, but you gain something else, and you learn to grow with it and expand.[6]

Success requires unbelievable persistence. But we *can* draw on each other's resources and we *can* become a caring, sharing family.

As happened in one family, "they shared with each other their worlds, and indeed each was enriched and expanded by the other."[7]

Shalom!—Beginnings

I have come that men may have life, and may have it in all its fullness"
(John 10:10).

L ife does become good again. Healing came, but it did take time.

One of the first "breakthroughs" for me in my *becoming* was when I took my wedding and engagement rings from my left hand and put them on my right hand. I was now "officially" single. At that time I also had my hair cut. Lin had wanted it long and it had been that way for several years. Now it was short again. The beginnings of the new me.

One day I woke up happy. I can't tell you when. But I realized I was happy again.

I had been to camp for a summer with the boys, initiating a new program in camping ministry. I had completed college. The family had taken up skiing. We were feeling good as a family. And I felt good about me.

Robert Benson, in his book *Come Share the Being*, tells of his son:

Let me brag a little—
I have a grandson named Robert Green Benson, III.
Now, in case you're not big on family trees
    that makes me Robert Green Benson, Sr.
And I have a son Robert Green Benson, Jr.
    and a grandson Robert Green Benson, III.

Before he was born we were duly notified
    that in the event the baby was a boy, he would be so named
        and we were to call him Robert.
Peering across the gap between the generations
 ˙I took this to mean that we were not to make the same mistake
    of re-using such terms as

Bobby or little Bobby or Baby Bobby—
    it was to be Robert.
It seemed like quite a handle to me
        for less than ten pounds of humanity—
it seemed very awkward to say, "Goochy-goochy" Robert.
But Robert it was—
    until somebody started calling him "Pookie"
    or just "Pook" for short.
Now Bobby sounds better to me than Pookie
        but then what do grandfathers know?

But a little while after Robert was born
    Tom, my ten-year-old, said to his mom,
"Robert sure is lucky."
            And Peg wanted to know why
            Robert was so lucky in Tom's mind.
"Because he gets to do all them new things."
            And now she wanted to know what all
            those new things were that Tom
            was referring to.
"Well," Tom began,
    "He's never climbed a tree
    or waded in the lake
        or run through a field
        or felt the wind in his face
        or ridden a bicycle—
        ALL THEM NEW THINGS."

And I was thinking later about all of God's children
    and about our life in the Spirit
and about all the wonderful surprises
and about all the wonderful surprises
and stupendous things He has for all of us to do
            and see
            and feel
            and be. . . .[1]

And that's where I was—beginning "all them new things"
and life was good.

A verse in Hebrews 10:39 says, "We have the faith to make
life our own." Not just for the hereafter, but faith for the now,
to make life something NOW. It reminds me of I Corinthians
3:9, "And you are God's garden." Here I am with the faith to
make life my own. I am God's garden. I can go into that garden
and not only look, but pick those flowers, make a bouquet or
a corsage, a thing of beauty because I have the faith to make life
my own! I am alive.

I don't know who figured the brick for my house, but he way
overfigured. Twelve years later I am still building flower beds and
sidewalks and patios out of those extra bricks. Peggy, the great

shopper, found some lovely old iron rail fence and I drove up to Lebanon and brought it home and made a pretty shrubbery and flower bed with the fence and the bricks out between some trees at the end of our house. When I made the bed, the bricks were over a foot or so from the trees, but those crazy trees grew over by my bricks. And give them another three or four years and they'll push my wall over. You'd think when you laid a bunch of heavy bricks around a tree, the tree wouldn't have a chance.

> But it just keeps pushing
> and shoving,
> it just keeps moving—
> it's just alive.

I know you've seen a sidewalk that a tree root has just picked up. Somebody poured the concrete and said, "Aw, don't worry about that root—this concrete's heavy." And the root said, "Aw, don't worry about that concrete—I'm alive," and now it's 8 to 2 in favor of the root.[2]

I was feeling alive, new, good about myself, and yet there had been a time when I wondered if I'd ever feel good again.

I was feeling like the writer of Hebrews in Hebrews 13:21: "And may he make of us what he would have us be. . . ." The process was begun and I knew it was continuing. I was becoming! In order for that process to continue, I knew I had to take some risks.

The little book, *Hope for the Flowers*, tells of caterpillars making caterpillar pillars, not knowing where they would lead, but joining the struggle to climb where everyone else seemed to be. Safety in numbers, I guess. Two caterpillars, Yellow and Stripe, meet and get involved. Their struggles are depicted in this excellent book.

Yellow says, "Tell me, sir, what is a butterfly?" "It's what you are meant to become."[3]

"How does one become a butterfly?" she asked pensively.

"You must want to fly so much that you are willing to give up being a caterpillar."[4]

To me, that spoke of risk. Then, "How could she risk the only life she knew?" . . . "What did she have to go on?—seeing another caterpillar who believed enough to make his own cocoon—and that peculiar hope which had kept her off the pillar and leapt within her when she heard about butterflies."[5]

"And Yellow decided to risk for a butterfly . . . saying, 'If I have inside me the stuff to make cocoons—maybe the stuff of butterflies is there, too.'"[6]

I guess I didn't want to sit around content to be a caterpillar when there was the possibility of a butterfly inside. I would have to risk making a cocoon and try for the butterfly. I had seen others do it. I had to risk giving up the known world of a caterpillar for the unknown of the butterfly. But others had tested it. Hope was there. Because of hope, I would take risks. "All them new things" were happening. I was feeling alive.

Part of risking and growing for me had to deal with expressing feelings. Real learning took place through an internship at a treatment center for alcoholics and drug users.

> October 5, 1976. I hesitate writing because there is so much to write. I am excited about what is happening to me! Today J. was having a bad time. Language is quite strong at those times! Gary Kern (counselor) suggested we give gifts to one another to change our tense emotions. J. refused to participate. After it was over, I told J. I wanted to give him a gift. He said he didn't want one. I said I still wanted to give him one and he repeated that he didn't want a gift. So I got up and went to J., held his hands and said, "J., I give you the gift of love and friendship and leadership," and squeezed his hands. He said, "Thank you," and grinned broadly! Gary said, "I thought you were going to kiss him"—so I did! *I shared a feeling!* And it felt good— doing what I wanted to do and not worrying about how I looked. And J. turned and gave a gift to someone else! Gary really affirmed me in this and thanked me. I feel full—to overflowing. When I prayed with Rob tonight, I prayed, "Thank you, Lord, for the excitement of life and for people who make it possible." And they don't even have to be Christians (common grace?). Feelings are gifts from God and can be used for Him and for me.

Emmett.

I was feeling good about life, about our family, about me. Maybe my biggest struggle was that I was enjoying being single. Emmett's wife, Darlene, had died and we began seeing each other. We had a lot in common. That's why others had us "matched" before we even began dating! We loved life. We were involved in some of the same organizations and committees. We had similar skills.

But Emmett had cancer.

> Saturday, February 13, 1977. I've been with Emmett every

night since Tuesday (oh, no, not on Wednesday). I just don't know how "uninvolved" I can be.

I found my journal centered a lot on Emmett's cancer.

Wednesday, February 16, 1977. I was on the verge of tears all through Bible study—just wondering what was best concerning Emmett and me. Plus that, when Emmett arrived back from the doctor, the news was obviously not good. We went into his office and I just cried. That night while praying, Rob prayed, "Thank You for Mom and Emmett and all You've done for them." And I cried again.

I wrote down some things to help me get things into perspective. Among them were some things regarding my involvement with Emmett—whether or not we should continue seeing each other. I was concerned for the boys, whether they should be subjected to another deep hurt. Cancer and future hurt were forever on my mind. But we still continued to date and I continued to back away when I found myself getting too close.

Then August came. It seemed that a mass had developed in Emmett's abdomen. Some of the tumors seemed to have shrunk while others had grown. Chemotherapy was working on some and not on others? It didn't make sense!

Tuesday, August 23, 1977. Yesterday I took Emmett to the hospital for his days of tests. Just an unsettled feeling sticking deep inside me.

Thursday, August 25, 1977. Tonight is something else! Because of the test results, Emmett will have surgery in the morning and there's that ominous feeling about. For all that I have insisted on not telling him that I love him, I sure do care a lot. He read from Psalm 116 in *Psalms Now:*

I know that God is here.
I know this because,
   my soul bare and body naked before Him,
   He looked upon me with love
      and responded to my cry for help.

There was a time when I didn't care!
I was not aware of any particular need for Him.
But then I hit bottom.
Death itself reached out to embrace me.
There was no one else to turn to.
I cried out to God in my desperation.

I could almost feel His invisible hand
   encircle me and draw me to Himself.

Now I am convinced.
God is here, and I shall trust Him forever.
I will no longer wait for pain or suffering
   to drive me to Him.
I will walk in His course for my life.
I am committed to His purposes,
   and I intend to carry out that commitment.

I can never repay God for His ever-present love.
I can only dedicate my life to praising Him
   and to serving Him wherever I may be.
I am His servant and His son; I shall love Him forever.
I shall proclaim to all the world: "God is in our midst."[7]

I am so glad God *is* in control even though at times I want to wonder about that.

Friday, August 26, 1977. Wow! Has today been draining. More than I realized. Emmett had surgery and Keith and I were with him for several hours. He was in so much pain he couldn't stand it. He'd say, "Hon, I don't know if I can make it through this." I was so tired—emotionally drained!

Tonight was better. The pain was bad but not excruciating, so there was a little visiting rather than watching him in pain.

Emmett asked tonight if this brought back memories. I said that memories of Lin weren't there so much but the "feelings" were there. Actually, I guess that would be the memories, too, even though I wasn't conscious of that.

Tuesday, September 6, 1977. A lot has gone on since August 26. The biggie is that there is *no clinical evidence of Hodgkin's!* Like Emmett told the doctor—I think this borders on the miraculous!

There was no more cancer!

It's amazing how quickly I learned what my true feelings were.

Shortly after Emmett got out of the hospital, we went to a jewelry store. He wanted to buy me a gift in celebration of "life." Wholeness of life.

There was a beautiful bracelet with diamonds on it (he had sold a house, made money on it, and wanted to blow it all!). But I saw a pewter butterfly, a lovely little thing. The jeweler couldn't believe that I would choose a pewter butterfly over an expensive bracelet. But the butterfly depicted life to me. That is what I wanted!

Thursday, September 22, 1977. Yesterday was Emmett's forty-ninth birthday. Tuesday I took him to the Fox and Hound restaurant. It was so neat giving him a picture of us and then to see his expression when he read the card I gave him telling him I loved him and would be proud to spend the rest of his birthdays with him.

Actually, I guess I proposed to him!

The next day, when asked what he got for his birthday, he responded with, "Nancy!"

We discussed when we would get married. We finally decided on January 5. *But* we were going on a tour to Israel that Emmett and our friend, Wes Forsline, were to lead. I was arranging rooming for the group. Emmett, being the only single man, would be alone the entire tour. As I was giving the rooming list to the travel agent, she said to me, "As long as you are engaged and planning on being married, why don't you get married in Israel?" Did that ever interest me! She checked on the possibility and within twenty minutes our January 5 date was changed to November 13, 1977! We would be married by the Sea of Galilee in Israel.

I wrote about our wedding in my journal.

November 14, 1977. I'll *never* be able to express my feelings about yesterday. I feel so much in love, so full of grace, so utterly happy and oozing with joy and spiritual well-being.

First thing in the morning, as we got on the bus, Solomon (the bus driver) was stringing flowers all over. It began as a day of celebration. Our visits to various sights might just as well have been excluded. Anticipation and excitement ruled the tour.

At noon, we ate at a Kibbutz where we changed clothes. And people began taking pictures—I mean everyone—even people from other countries.

Then we went—dressed up—and carrying roses that Solomon rounded up somewhere (when asked where he got them, he said, "Don't ask!") for more pictures and to an absolutely beautiful spot on the Sea of Galilee, Gromosan, where our wedding took place. Our dear friend, Wes Forsline, led the service.

We had a vocal recording by Lisa, Emmett's secretary, to begin the service. Wes then began setting the tone for a memorable wedding:

"Nancy and Emmett, what an absolutely beautiful thing to participate in today. Your wedding here on the shore of the Sea of Galilee at a spot where we know Jesus walked.

"I am moved deeply, for I know how much this means to both of you, for you have gone through the experiences of life over which you could write many chapters, and you have. Now, another chapter is being written because of the gift of God's grace to both of you. What an absolute delight."

Wes then read I Corinthians 13, the closing words being "In a word, there are three things that last forever. Faith, hope, and love. And when all else is gone, love will still be."

Gordon Krantz then sang "I Walked Today Where Jesus Walked." By then, my eyes were brimming.

Emmett and I wrote our own vows and shared them with each other.

Wes prayed: "O Sovereign Lord, God, in the name of the Living Christ, whose presence is now here, whose Spirit fills the earth as you have filled these moments, we commit to You Emmett and Nancy.

"Up the road of their tomorrows lead them. Take them by the hand and bless them in the ministry that shall be given to our world through their lives, through the lives that they care for intimately, the lives that they shall influence.

"We ask your abundant blessing upon their children, upon their future, upon their days together as a gift of God with all the surprises of grace that come day by day.

"May they find above all that You are the constant and absolute factor that holds them together and gives them strength and purpose for each day and for each tomorrow. Take them by the hand, our Lord. Lead them, until one day we shall know as we are known, and we shall stand in the mighty presence of God and we shall know him forever, in a world where all the shadows are forever gone and we live and love as Christ our Lord.

"In whose matchless name we lift our humble prayer.
                    "Amen."

As he prayed, we wept.

After being pronounced husband and wife, we sang, "To God Be the Glory," and then served communion to the others, singing "Amazing Grace." We closed the service with a Hebrew song, "Havano Shalom Alahem" (Broad Peace to All).

That night I felt so happy, so absolutely satisfied with life—complete—Shalom!

We began our journey together. We had good days, happy, full days; and some days, I've had to say again, "More cotton, Lord."

A year and a half after we were married, on Easter Sunday, 1978, Steve and Rob were baptized. I had asked our pastor if Emmett could baptize the boys. Before the baptismal service, the pastor asked Emmett to lead in prayer. Because it was Easter Sunday, Emmett mentioned in his prayer that "after crosses comes resurrection."

Both boys went into the baptistry with Emmett. He talked to them. They gave their testimonies of receiving Jesus Christ as their Savior and Lord—Steve, praying with Lin when he was only seven; Rob, praying with me the year Lin died. Emmett went on, "Had Lindon lived he would be baptizing the boys now. I am happy I can be here now baptizing them." It was a moving experience.

After the service, several from the church came to me saying, "Do you realize what day this is? Five years ago today, Lin was buried from the church."

Yes, after crosses comes resurrection. Lin was buried. The boys were buried with Christ, baptized into the newness of life.

Emmett and I and the boys are establishing a new life together; he is cancer-free and healthy! We continue to do impulsive things that puzzle the onlooker.

Life is good.

The last of my life is more blest than the first.

LaChayim—To Life!

Shalom!

Appendix

INFORMATION FCR SURVIVORS

(Information of this type, revised as circumstances change, should be made a part of one's personal papers, filed in an agreed-upon place. This printed page itself is not to be filled out and filed.)

Key Persons to Be Notified
1. Pastor _____Phone Number _____
2. Doctor _____Phone Number _____
3. Funeral Home _____Phone Number _____
4. Executor of Will _____Phone Number _____

Relatives and Friends to Be Notified
Names, addresses, phone numbers

_____

_____

_____

Insurance Policies

Company   Policy Number   Amount   Agent

_____

_____

Veterans' Records:
Identification Number _____VA Office to Notify _____
_____ Location of Discharge Papers _____
Social Security Number: _____
Pension Benefits from employer—who should be notified: _____
Location of Will: _____
Location of Safe Deposit Box: _____
Attorney: Name, address, phone number _____
Bank Accounts: Name of bank, type of account

_____

_____

Outstanding Loans and Credit Obligations

_____

_____

121

Cemetery: Name, location, lot and deed numbers

_____

My Personal Preferences
    Autopsy: Yes _____No _____
    Funeral service from the church: Yes _____No _____
    Burial _____Mausoleum _____Cremation _____Other _____
    Memorial gifts should be encouraged for:

_____
_____

Special Requests: _____
_____
_____

Biographical Information
    Born (place and date of birth)_____
    Name of father _____
    Maiden name of mother _____
    Date *Baptized* _____Date *Confirmed* _____
    For married persons: place and date of marriage: _____

_____

    My signature _____Date _____
    Address _____
    "You are not your own; you were bought with a price. So glorify God in your body" (1 Cor. 6:19, 20).

Printed in U.S.A.

7-65-150M

Submitted by

**Commission on Research
and Social Action**

**The American Lutheran Church
422 South Fifth Street
Minneapolis, Minnesota 55415
July 1965**

Notes

Chapter 1

[1] Nancy Karo, *Adventure in Dying* (Chicago: Moody Press, 1976), p. 23. Copyright 1976. Moody Press, Moody Bible Institute of Chicago. Used by permission.

[2] *Ibid.*, p. 85.

[3] *Ibid.*, p. 86.

Chapter 2

[1] Larry K. May, "Through the Valley of Death," *Pulpit Digest*, May, 1964, p. 50.

[2] Karen Kaiser Clark, *Where Have All the Children Gone? Gone to Grown-Ups, Everyone* (St. Paul: The Center for Executive Planning, Inc., 1977). Reprinted by permission of The Center for Executive Planning, Inc., 355 Cimarron Road, St. Paul, MN 55124.

[3] Leslie Weatherhead, *Why Do Men Suffer?* (Nashville: Abingdon Press, 1963), pp. 134-135. Copyright renewal 1963 by Leslie D. Weatherhead. Used by permission of the publisher, Abingdon Press.

Chapter 3

[1] Philip W. Williams, *When a Loved One Dies* (Minneapolis: Augsburg Publishing House, 1976), p. 31.

[2] Leslie S. Brandt, *Psalms Now* (St. Louis: Concordia Publishing House, 1973), p. 215. Used by permission.

[3] Richard Krebs, *Alone Again* (Minneapolis: Augsburg Publishing House, 1978), p. 99.

[4] *Ibid.*

[5] Alvin Rogness, *Appointment with Death* (Nashville: Thomas Nelson, Inc., 1972).

Chapter 4

[1] Edgar N. Jackson, *You and Your Grief* (Great Neck, New York: Channel Press, Inc., 1961), p. 17. Reprinted by permission of the publisher, E. P. Dutton, from *You and Your Grief* by Edgar Jackson. Copyright © 1962, 1961 by Edgar N. Jackson. (A Hawthorne Book).

[2] Philip W. Williams, *When a Loved One Dies* (Minneapolis: Augsburg Publishing House, 1976), p. 11.

[3] *Ibid.*, p. 23.

⁴Mary Peacock, "The Importance of Crying," *MS.*, Vol. 7, no. 12 (June, 1980), p. 45.
⁵Joseph Bayly and Dean Merrill, *If I Should Die Before I Wake* (Elgin, Ill.: David C. Cook Publishing Co., 1976), p.14.
⁶Jackson, *For the Living*, p. 29.
⁷*Ibid.*
⁸Williams, *op. cit.*, p. 57.

Chapter 5

¹Nancy Karo, *Adventure in Dying* (Chicago: Moody Press, 1976), p. 87. Copyright 1976. Moody Press, Moody Bible Institute of Chicago. Used by permission.
²*Ibid.*, pp. 88, 89, 90.
³William Clyde Donald II, "The Therapy of Grief," *History of the Michigan Funeral Directors Association*, Lansing, 1960.
⁴Charles Bauchmann, "Ministering to the Grief Sufferer," *Successful Pastoral Counseling* (Englewood Cliffs, New Jersey: Prentice-Hall, Inc., 1964), p. 2.
⁵Edgar N. Jackson, *For the Living* (Des Moines: Channel Press, 1963), p. 41.
⁶Roy Pearson, "Let's Be Sensible About Funerals," *Church Management*, January, 1960.
⁷Bauchmann, *op. cit.*, p. 2.
⁸Edgar N. Jackson, *You and Your Grief* (Great Neck, New York: Channel Press, Inc., 1961), p. 42. Reprinted by permission of the publisher, E. P. Dutton, from *You and Your Grief* by Edgar Jackson. Copyright © 1962, 1961 by Edgar N. Jackson. (A Hawthorne Book).
⁹Seymour Shubin, "In Time of Sorrow: The Gift of Your Presence," *Reader's Digest*, June, 1964. Reprinted by permission from *Guideposts Magazine*, published by Guideposts Associates, Inc., Carmel, New York 10512.

Chapter 6

¹Leslie Weatherhead, *Why Do Men Suffer?* (Nashville: Abingdon Press, 1963), p. 78. Copyright renewal 1963 by Leslie D. Weatherhead. Used by permission of the publisher, Abingdon Press.

Chapter 7

¹Bob Benson, *Come Share the Being* (Nashville: Impact Books, 1974), pp. 44, 45.

Chapter 8

¹From the song "Jesus Walked This Lonesome Valley" by Erna Moorman. © Copyright 1976 by Fred Bock Music Company. All rights reserved. Used by permission.
²Phil Donahue, "Coping Alone," *Philadelphia Inquirer*, April 1, 1980, as reprinted from Phil Donahue and Company, *Donahue, My Own Story* (New York: Simon & Schuster, 1980).
³Philip W. Williams, *When a Loved One Dies* (Minneapolis: Augsburg Publishing House, 1976), pp. 49, 50.

Chapter 9

¹Linda Bird Francke, Pamela Ellis Simons, Pamela Abramson Marsha Zabarsky, Janet Huck, and Lisa Whitman, "The Children of Divorce," *Newsweek*, February 11, 1980, pp. 58, 59.
²Ruth Roosevelt and Jeannette Lofas, *Living in Step* (New York: McGraw-Hill Book Company, 1976), pp. 100, 101. Copyright © 1976 by Ruth Roosevelt and Jeannette Lofas. Reprinted with permission of Stein and Day Publishers.
³Francke *op. et. al., cit.*, pp. 58-60.
⁴*Ibid.*, p. 62.
⁵*Ibid.*, p. 61.

[6] *Ibid.*

Chapter 10

[1] Richard Krebs, *Alone Again* (Minneapolis: Augsburg Publishing House, 1978), p. 96.

[2] Phil Donahue, "Coping Alone," *Philadelphia Inquirer*, April 1, 1980, as reprinted from Phil Donahue and Company, *Donahue, My Own Story* (New York: Simon & Schuster, 1980).

[3] Harold Ivan Smith, "Sex and Singleness the Second Time Around," *Christianity Today*, May 25, 1979, p. 18, as adapted from *A Part of Me Is Missing* (Eugene, Oregon: Harvest House Publishers, 1979). Copyright, 1979, Harvest House Publishers, 1075 Arrowsmith, Eugene, Oregon 97402.

Chapter 11

[1] "Eliza's House," *McCall's* magazine, vol. 107, no. 1, p. 79.

[2] Phil Donahue, "Coping Alone," *Philadelphia Inquirer*, April 1, 1980, as reprinted from Phil Donahue and Company, *Donahue, My Own Story* (New York: Simon and Schuster, 1980).

[3] From Robert A. Raines, "This Fruitful Season," in *Lord, Could You Make It a Little Better?* (Waco: Word Books, 1972), p. 71. Copyright 1972; used by permission of Word Books, Publisher, Waco, Texas 76796.

[4] Edgar N. Jackson, *You and Your Grief* (Great Neck, New York: Channel Press, Inc., 1961), p. 33. Reprinted by permission of the publisher, E. P. Dutton, from *You and Your Grief* by Edgar Jackson. Copyright © 1962, 1961 by Edgar N. Jackson. (A Hawthorne Book).

Chapter 12

[1] Darrell Sifford, *Philadelphia Inquirer*, September 14, 1980.

[2] Brenda Maddox, *Half-Parent* (New York: Signet Books, 1975), p. 7.

[3] Ruth Roosevelt and Jeannette Lofas, *Living in Step* (New York: McGraw-Hill Book Company, 1976), p. 111. Copyright © 1976 by Ruth Roosevelt and Jeannette Lofas. Reprinted with permission of Stein and Day Publishers.

[4] *Ibid.*

[5] Richard Krebs, *Alone Again* (Minneapolis: Augsburg Publishing House, 1978), p. 92.

[6] Roosevelt and Lofas, *op. cit.*, p. 127.

[7] *Ibid.*, p. 40.

Chapter 13

[1] Bob Benson, *Come Share the Being* (Nashville: Impact Books, 1974), pp. 36, 37.

[2] *Ibid.*, p. 33.

[3] Trina Paulus, *Hope for the Flowers* (Paramus, New Jersey: Paulist Press, 1972), p. 70. Reprinted from *Hope for the Flowers* by Trina Paulus, © 1972 by Trina Paulus. Used by permission of Paulist Press.

[4] *Ibid.*, p. 75.

[5] *Ibid.*, p. 80.

[6] *Ibid.*, p. 84.

[7] Leslie F. Brandt, *Psalms Now* (St. Louis: Concordia Publishing House, 1973), p. 122. Used by permission.

Bibliography and Suggested Readings

Bayly, Joseph and Merrill, Dean, *If I Should Die Before I Wake.* Elgin, Illinois: David C. Cook Publishing Co., 1976.

Benson, Bob, *Come Share the Being.* Nashville: John T. Benson Publishing Co., 1974.

Berson, Barbara, and Bova, Ben, *Survival Guide for the Suddenly Single.* New York: St. Martin's Press, 1974.

Clark, Karen, *Where Have All the Children Gone? Gone to Grownups, Everyone.* St. Paul: Center for Executive Planning, Inc., 1977.

Donald, William Clyde, II, "The Therapy of Grief," *History of the Michigan Funeral Directors Association.* Lansing, Michigan, 1960.

Ellisen, Stanley A., *Divorce and Remarriage in the Church.* Grand Rapids: Zondervan Corporation, 1977.

Francke, Linda Bird; Simons, Pamela Ellis; Abramson, Pamela; Zabarsky, Marsha; Huck, Janet; and Whitman, Lisa, "The Children of Divorce," *Newsweek,* February 11, 1980.

Grollman, Earl A., Editor, *Explaining Death to Children.* Boston: Beacon Press, 1969.

Grollman, Earl A., *Living When a Loved One Has Died.* Boston: Beacon Press, 1977.

Jackson, Edgar N., *For the Living.* Des Moines, Iowa: Channel Press, The Meredith Publishing Company, 1963.

Jackson, Edgar N., *The Many Faces of Grief.* Nashville: Abingdon Press, 1977.

Jackson, Edgar N., *Understanding Grief.* New York: Nashville: Abingdon Press, 1957.

Jackson, Edgar N., *You and Your Grief*. Great Neck, New York: Channel Press, Inc., 1961.

Karo, Nancy, *Adventure in Dying*. Chicago: Moody Press, 1976.

Klopfenstein, Janette, *Tell Me About Death, Mommy*. Scottsdale, Pennsylvania: Herald Press, 1977.

Krebs, Richard, *Alone Again*. Minneapolis: Augsburg Publishing House, 1978.

Kübler-Ross, Elisabeth, *Death, the Final Stage of Growth*. Englewood Cliffs, New Jersey: Prentice-Hall, Inc., 1975.

Kübler-Ross, Elisabeth, *On Death and Dying*. New York: The Macmillan Company, 1970.

Maddox, Brenda, *Half-Parent*. New York: Signet Books, The New American Library, 1975.

May, Larry K., "Through the Valley of Death," *Pulpit Digest*, Long Island, New York, May 1964.

Paulus, Trina, *Hope for the Flowers*. Paramus, New Jersey: Paulist/ Newman Press, 1972.

Peacock, Mary, "The Importance of Tears," *MS.*, vol. 7, no. 12, June, 1980.

Pearson, Roy, "Let's Be Sensible About Funerals," *Church Management*, January, 1960.

Phillips, Carolyn, *Our Family Got a Divorce*. Glendale, California: Gospel Light Publications, 1979.

Powell, John, *Fully Human, Fully Alive*. Niles, Illinois: Argus Communications, 1976.

Powell, John, *Why Am I Afraid to Tell You Who I Am?* Niles, Illinois: Argus Communications, 1969.

Roosevelt, Ruth, and Lofas, Jeannette, *Living in Step*. New York: Stein and Day, 1976.

Tournier, Paul, *Escape from Loneliness*. Philadelphia: The Westminster Press, 1962.

Williams, Philip W., *When a Loved One Dies*. Minneapolis: Augsburg Publishing House, 1976.

White, John, *Parents in Pain*. Downers Grove, Illinois: Inter-Varsity Press, 1979.

Weatherhead, Leslie D., *Why Do Men Suffer?* Nashville: Abingdon Press, 1963.